"Sexy Food for Singles"

by

Lorraine

Romantic Tips ...
How to Be Terrific

Published by
Sundae Publications

"Sexy Food for Singles"

by

Lorraine

Copyright ©2000.

Published in the United States of America by

Sundae Publications

70 Winter Street

Wellesley, Massachusetts 02481-2175

1-877-SexyFood ... Toll Free

ISBN #0-9700110-0-8

Library of Congress no. 00-090633

Cover Design

Entire creative concept for book cover and illustration by Lorraine

Art Work
by Mark Steele
www.marksteeleart.com

Book cover
By Bruce Jones Design, Inc.
www.bjdesign.com/bjdesign.html

<u>Thank you</u> ... <u>Thank you</u> ...

<u>Thank you</u> ... <u>Thank you</u> ...

Dorothea S. Piranian

Jessie Janjigian von Hippel

Lisa Smith, *Editorial Services and Typesetting*

Hans, *Creative Computer Consultant*

❖❖❖❖❖❖❖❖❖❖❖❖❖❖❖❖❖❖❖❖❖❖❖❖❖❖❖❖

Dan Poynter's Book

Richard Simonian, Esq.

Armand H. Andreassian

Garo Papazian

Romantic Gifts
www.me2you.com

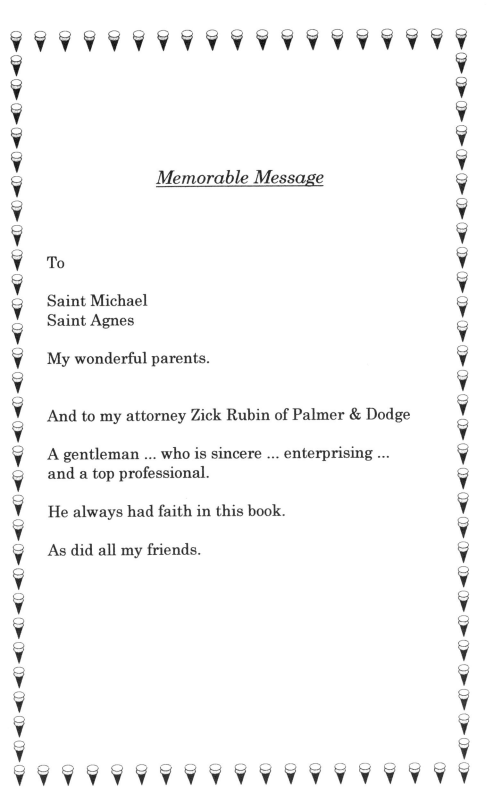

Memorable Message

To

Saint Michael
Saint Agnes

My wonderful parents.

And to my attorney Zick Rubin of Palmer & Dodge

A gentleman ... who is sincere ... enterprising ...
and a top professional.

He always had faith in this book.

As did all my friends.

TABLE OF CONTENTS

"*I know. But I think I can change him.*"

CUTTING THE MUSTARD

This book is novel ... comic ... and unique ... because the author is.

Is the author conceited? Yes! But even <u>more</u> ... confident and charming.

You should see her ... a calorie-counting workshop would love her for a client ... so would a plastic surgeon ... (maybe someday).

Yet ... she is extremely popular with several ... single ... successful ... sophisticated ... decent ... wonderful ... <u>vital</u> men!

Ask any of her 30 or more male friends. Ask any of those hundreds of women and dozens of men who ask her advice ... and <u>always</u> say ... "You're 100% right" ... or "Right on."

Ask the author ... she'll tell you ... "If I can do 'it' ... so can you!"

"It" didn't just happen. When she was in high school ... there was no one more awkward ... introverted ... and unpopular with the fellows.

She used to scream ... cry and scream some more ... because she wanted to be a cute ... perky blonde.

Lorraine had super parents ... <u>the</u> best ... (both of Armenian descent) ... who taught her values. Her Mother was president of every club she belonged to ... her Father ... struggled to be a successful ice cream manufacturer.

Which reminds her of a story told to her by Arthur Gregorian ... a famous rug dealer. Her Father was to purchase an oriental from him ... and wasn't happy ... stating the rug designs weren't perfect. Mr. Gregorian mentioned ... *The rugs were handmade ... what if I said your vanilla ice cream wasn't perfect.*

In college, Lorraine realized that no one is perfect ... and was going to lick that cone ... and not melt away! From being plain vanilla ... to hot fudge!

We all have an ice cream flavor in us ... with tasty toppings.

But you must have the right recipes ... with surprise sauces ... flavorings ... ingredients ... utensils ... delicate dressings ... from flat pancakes to puffy popovers ... with succulent syrup and butter that melts in <u>their</u> mouth.

Be an appealing appetizer ... exciting entrée ... They just can't wait for the dessert!

You and Lorraine will shape a special sundae together.

"Now let's talk about you!"

Chapter I

A TEMPTING ... DELICIOUS DISH!

That's you! Yesssss ... you!

Dream and schemes for both sexes ... who are single ... widowed ... separated ... divorced ... married ... <u>anyone</u> of adult age!

It doesn't matter whether you're heavy ... homespun ... or over the hill ... you <u>can</u> be a hallmark ... How? Stop being ho-hum ... hollow and humble! "Make" it happen ... instead of hoping ... be happy ... instead of hapless.

We're all of the same stock ... sweet ... sour ... spicy and salty.

It's up to you to create your own concoction ... Add your own seasonings ... so your dish will be more delicious and different and not cafeteria style!

Everyone will want <u>your</u> recipes ... your secret ingredients ... always a surprise. You'll have so many originals ... <u>you</u> could write a book.

As my dramatic teacher used to say ... *Spread it ... darlings ... spread it.*

Breakfast ... brunch ... banquet ... You will digest it all ... because you're going to be a treat!

But not if you're in any of these slices ... no matter what age ... no matter which gender ...

1. You can't be bothered with delicate ... delectable appetizers ... too much work "doing" a dish that is stirring and worth waiting for.

   Just stuff yourself with meat and potatoes ... right to the dessert ... get it on quickly ... or not at all.

2. Or you're stale ... crusty ... toast ... a puddinghead ... a morsel who fritters away ... and blames everyone except yourself.

3. Do you fantasize you're a peach or a pear ... but really only the fuzz ... and not a pair?

You:
Mirror ... mirror ... on the wall
Who's the fairest of them all?

Mirror:
I've told you before ... You're not even on my list.

Someday ... you won't have to ask ... you'll <u>know</u> ... you're sexy ... sexier ... sexiest of them all!

Men must be hot to be cool ... Women must be cool to be hot!

I'm not biting ... about food ... but passion fruit.

I'll show you not only how to prepare one ... but how to <u>be</u> one! Peaches flambé all the way.

Food cannot only be sexy ... but funny ... I'll fill you full of fancy frosting and punch.

Sweet and strong ... You will know your onions and when to eat them or not.

But hold the onions.

First ... don't fantasize!

Get real ... get on with it ... and you've got "it"!

Ask yourself, are you ready? Are you raw ... rare ... medium ... or well done? None of these should be on the menu.

The proof is in the pudding.

1. Be ready to mushroom
2. Want moxie
3. Make from scratch
4. Pour on the sauce
5. Turn over slowly
6. Feel your oats
7. Hash it over
8. Blend in
9. Eat humble pie
10. Say cheese ... most important

Botticelli isn't a wine, you jinnins! Botticelli's a cheese.
—Punch

He that is of merry heart hath a continual feast.
—The Bible

You can't make an omelet without breaking eggs.
—Proverb

Your shell will protect ... but also you must show what's inside. Will you be moist ... dry... beaten?

Are you hard-boiled ... scrambled ... sunny side up ... poached ... rotten ... fried ... loose ... cracked ... deviled?

Do you blend and mix with other fixings? Does it enhance your flavors when you're spiced up?

Yes! Yes! Yes!!!!

As you may have guessed ... one is to cook up a storm.

Sure ... the currant today is raisin' cane on the Internet ... ordering edibles ... having them delivered ... putting it away ... or before you arrive ... having the soup on.

Does that turn you on ... or turn the tables?

Auntie Mame hit the spot when she said ...

Life is a banquet, and most poor suckers are starving to death.
> —Betty Comden
> Adolph Green

If your cake is upside down ... you can still cover it with delicious icing.

Look at you! So you're a lemon ... hot dog ... or a sweet potato ... So what?

The crackerjack chefs are constantly breaking <u>new</u> grounds ... you dish it out, too.

Fresh food should be devoured now! So if you don't want to be wilted ... bottled ... canned ... or frozen out ... feast one's fill now. No matter what age or who you are.

No brush-off ... If you don't give a fig ... others will poach on your parade ... and the plums of life will pass you by.

A disaster can be a delight and delectable. I'll give you the scoop on that subject later.

Peach Melba ... Melba Toast ... Turkey Tetrazzini ... were named after opera stars ... There are others. Create your own concoctions. You're famous to you!

Simple or sophisticated ... make ... fix ... prepare ... and name the treat after yourself or your beau.

Samples:

Bob's Oysters in Bed
Judy's Jeweled Dessert
Timothy's Perfect Popovers
Monica's Glazed Cherries

Proven methods doled out throughout the generations have shown to smack your lips over their aroma and your appetite for more. You can digest these techniques ... then add or subtract your own touch ... A dash there ... a sprinkle there ... and voilà ... you've become a gourmet.

After a good dinner, one can forgive anybody, even one's own relations.
                                                    —Oscar Wilde

Be ginger and snap to it.

Most methods I toss out may not be your cup of tea. In fact, you might think them half-baked or dippy.

A greased pan gets the batter ... hits a home run ... and wins the "game."

You, too, can realize you have relish ... you're a great catch ... and ...

You are what you eat and cook.

Timing ... Toss well ... Treat ... not Trick ...

Lower the heat when your kettle is boiling over ... It makes a mess ... Store in a cool place.

Pavarotti is not vain, but conscious of being unique.
                                        —Peter Ustinov

Don't be yourself!

Your features are teeming with traits and winning ways ... Be awake ... be aware and work at it.

One favorite friend cited that he never knew how I would greet him ... whether I'd pounce ... do a jig ... make foolish faces ... screech 'You're three minutes late ... leave!' ... or cuddle and chip ... 'Kitchy-kitchy koo.'

He loved every minute of it ... *It keeps me on my toes.*

As a matter of fact ... I do that with most men. And they love it. Yes ... they do.

And do I leave a message on the telephone like any average individual ... No way!

1. (Cutely) 'Tweet ... tweet ... tweet ... call me tout de suite ... (briskly) or you're mincemeat!'

2. 'It's meeee!!'

3. (Singing) 'I'm called little buttercup ... and you're my little teacup!'

4. (Singing) 'Oh, where, oh, where ... are you?'

5. 'You'll nevvvvver guess who <u>this</u> is!'

You may picture this as too silly for words ... <u>it</u> <u>is</u>!

You also wouldn't perceive to make a fool of yourself.

'Tis no shame, to have been foolish; the shame lies in not having cut the folly short.
                    —Horace

He who lives without folly is less wise than he believes.
                    —Le Roche Foucauld

He does it with better grace, but I do it more natural.
                    —Shakespeare

Naturally ... it's impressive ... because I used my imagination.

I'm never ignored
Because I'm never bored

They know who meeee is ... they tweet ... tweet, too ... sing or leave their own clever message.

To think anyone I know is a nerd
Is utterly ... absolutely absurd.

Some rules say ... don't call or bother them ...

<u>Isn't</u> <u>that</u> <u>the</u> <u>idea</u>? I call men constantly ... and never feel
I'm doing the chasing ... It's clear to my friends ... I'm not.
They encourage me to contact them.

Time and tide wait for no man ... (or woman).
                                        —Proverb

Call continually or occasionally ... it depends what rapport
you have with the fellow or gal.

Toute le monde loves attention. But don't be a pest ...
pessimistic ... or put them or yourself on a pedestal.

As you become confident and a connoisseur ... you'll realize
that romance won't be by chance ... if you're creative and
comical. If you make them feel comfortable ... you've got it
made ... ready to serve.

Wear many harlequin ... hilarious hats ... but not a high ...
or hard hat. And hiding under them is not reliable ... nor
under the sheets ... tout de suite ... I did say ... tout de <u>sweet</u>!

Instead of being a virtuoso, the trend today is virtue ... oh ...
so what!

Instead of magnifying with magnetism ... magic ... and
slowly dropping ... your seven veils ... <u>one</u> at a time ... or
making your moves subtly ...

Today ... it's open ... sex ... for me ... and tipping your hand ...
instead of your hat. Oh ... hum!

It takes time to become a virtuoso. Tighten your strings ... and you won't be so high-strung.

Lead the parade ... swing your baton ... blow the trumpets ... bang the drums ... toot the flute ... but in harmony ... Let others join your cheers.

Keep in mind ... Sometimes the band doesn't "play" ... they just step ahead ... together. The tip is ... <u>together</u>. Never treat men/women like adversaries ... and you'll get a great treat.

Love and life isn't a kazoo where the melody or menu is quick. This noisemaking toy also has a harsh sound and could perform off key.

Dance a different tune ... the bolero instead of the boogaloo! Start the <u>ball</u> rolling!

I went to a social soirée where most of the music was rock 'n' roll. I burst forth with my boa and began a conga line. Was it a sockeroo ... neeeeed you ask?

Was also a smash ... (definitely ... not smashed) ... with a fellow when I pulled at his formal tie ... He kept in step ... as we waltzed and sang down the street. Others in our group quickly joined in.

A while back ... I went to the Riviera. Most gals were topless or in skimpy bikinis. One guess ... who stood out in her one-piece black lace bathing suit.

Can you picture me standing in line like a statue at the bank ... supermarket ... wedding reception ... theatre ... or being solemn in a hospital or nursing home?

When you're chatty and cheerful and launch laughter ... even to strangers ... who need their spirits lifted ... you will develop a domino effect.

This is the jet age ... zing ... zoom ... and zip into action! If you're genuine ... gregarious ... giving ... and "good" ... you don't have to be galley-proof ... prosperous ... well proportioned ... to <u>be</u> a gala.

But don't be so far out ... that you won't be "in"... by wearing a tutu at the Ritz ... Do a ballet at the Hard Rock Café ... Swim to the bolero wearing only a sombrero at the beach ... or sporting a clown's garb at the gym.

Though who knows ... I've noticed several buffoons swinging on the bars ... or trying to swing at bars. Nooooo ... you will never see me do the bar scene ... I <u>spotted</u> them ... That set will never change ... They are always so so-so ... so-and-sos ... plus full of pistachios ... too much salt and shell.

He can compress the most words into the smallest ideas better than any man I ever met.
                                        —Abraham Lincoln

Give out ... and they'll give in.

Flirting with a fantasy is just floating ... instead ... fling forward.

Recently ... invited five fellows and four gals to a tennis match ... all Dutch treat.

I designed the evening.

1. Five were to meet at my home at 5:00 p.m. <u>sharp</u> ... otherwise!!! They all came 30-45 minutes ... <u>early</u>.

2. They were to bring goodies ... for a treat after tennis. Oh ... the shrimp ... salmon paté ... (a fellow's specialty) ... grape leaves ... pies ... much more.

Boston cream pie is not my favorite ... but the dessert a good friend brought ... from one of the best bakeries ... Oh boy! He knew I'd love it. So creamy ... delicate ... smooth ... squeezed right down ... You wanted more.

Naturallllly ... a good time was had by all ... I don't mix with sours.

During the intervals ... at the tennis game ... we discussed the gathering at my home. A gentleman ... stranger to us all ... wanted to come! I found out it was his birthday.

In my Marlene Dietrich voice ... I sang "Happy Birthday." He and I enjoyed it ... but what surprised me ... was that <u>over</u> <u>50</u> people were listening! They <u>clapped</u> ... <u>cheered</u> and <u>chuckled</u> ... in <u>unison</u>. During the evening ... my friends kept mentioning that incident.

What are <u>you</u> waiting for? Stop being stale and stagnant ... leaning back in your comfy chair.

Start sitting on the <u>edge</u> of your chair ... raring to listen ... bursting with impressions and opinions ... and ready to spring up and out into song.

Socially ... business ... or kind service ... enthusiasm ... expression ... and energy ... will bring results.

<u>Men</u>: You're a flat tire with ...
1. How do I get out of this bad scene?
2. All women are only interested in a career.
3. They always want to spend my money.
4. No old-fashioned girls anymore.
5. I like them hot.
6. They don't care for me ... only themselves.

<u>Women</u>: You're dry as dust when you say ...
1. All the good men are taken.
2. They only want thirty-year-olds.
3. How did she get him?
4. Why did he leave me?
5. What can I do?
6. Where can I meet them?

So <u>many</u> ... want <u>one</u> formula ... <u>There</u> <u>are</u> <u>a</u> <u>baker's</u> <u>dozen</u>.

What have you done to improve yourself ... to charm ... capture ... conquer ... or change yourself creatively ... so they know you are <u>the</u> one!

100% of the time ... the answer is <u>nothing</u> or not very much!

Before you know ... you must be in the know about where and who you are.

First of all ... admit that it's your own fault.

Don't say ... *Er* or *What the hell do you mean?*

Rather, swear after you read my book ... never to ask anyone again.

Your personality will be so paramount ... people will think you're a star ... or someone special ... because you are!

Go from your regular route ... to a challenging <u>cause</u>way ... It might be bumpy with many curves ... and hills ... or seem like you're going around in circles ... but if you map it out ... have an itinerary ... you'll be on the right road.

In other words ... work ... work ... work ... work ... work ... work ...

You knew there was a catch ... but not if you want to be caught.

Others did to be tops. Put in as much energy in your character as you did in school ... and your profession.

Didn't you work hard to acquire a degree or a career? Didn't you become excited? You earned it. You knew you had to grow and develop.

Too many are commanding at the computer ... searching ... scanning ... and touching the right keys.

Welllll?

If you use your imagination ... they'll imagine your image important.

Savoir-faire ... and savoir-vivre.

No tricks ... just play your cards right ... into their arms ... by realizing it isn't the luck of the draw ... but skill in the technique in the dealing and winning.

1. There must be chemistry between you ... even a speck ... otherwise ... forget it.

2. Discover their hobbies ... dreams ... sports ... social life ... talents ... such as playing an instrument ... painting ... gardening ... inventions ... plus their professional world.

3. Perform a project together ... more later.

These are just sample ... simple ... snap ideas ... Read on ... MacDuff ... read on.

Courtship has flip-flopped ... Formal out ... casual in.

Like:
Red wine with fish
Wearing shorts ... no tie or hat to church.

How amused and annoyed I was ... when I first saw the young cross-bearer in church with his formal habit, donning dirty old sneakers. Now ... I'm used to it.

But never ... never ... never ... be used to lending or giving money to your "friend." You know what Judge Judy thinks about that.

Or scouring ... sweeping ... cleaning ... cooking ... without any returns ... so <u>many</u> times it can ricochet, and <u>their</u> response goes from sweet to sour.

Dates can be hot ... cold ... or dippy.

He's nicely dressed ... So is she.
He's on his best behavior ... So is she.
He takes her to a refined restaurant ... She loves it.
The conversation is pleasing and polite.
The food could be the worst ... Neither complain.
He wants a goodnight kiss or more.

She does or doesn't. If she doesn't ... he'll certainly try again ... or won't bother.
And so on and on and on!

Dullsville ... diluted!

What do I do? My currents are a tidal wave ... a bolt of lightning ... a twister ...

Cautious ... but catching! Charging ... not coy.

Forward ... yes!

Be forward ... no!

Sometimes I greet someone new with ... 'I hate your tie.' 'I just adorrrrre your haircut' ... or bark at him for any reason ... You can't chew out someone you've never met.

Fighting for fun.

They always break up ... and it breaks the ice.

Men:
Please never say you hate her dress. She'll throw it at you ... (and not the dress) ... though you wouldn't mind.

And for heaven's sake ... check out those clichés — *Where have you been all my life? ... How about it? ... Of all the joints .... Hello! My name is* _____.

How hip ... that ought to send her hopping ... to someone else!

A heartwarming look with a long ... loving handshake is lasting.

Praise them ... and pat yourself on the back ... but not too plummy.

The more you have ... the more they want.

Women:
Not only are men charged up when you are a challenge ... but when you take charge and dictate conditions.
More than a sprinkling of gals conclude that this course is too assertive and aggressive. They're the ones who sit and stew.
A greased pan gets the batter. If you don't go to bat ... someone else will pinch ... hit.

An international businessman declared ... *You don't say 'May I' ... You don't ask ... You order and we obey.* Another international executive walked in ... *That's Lorraine.*

Then ... we all went to church together to hear the *Messiah.*

I fan with flair ... flavor and femininity.

Their favors?

1. Still another international entrepreneur volunteered ... and saved thousands of dollars for me on a car.

2. Another ... brought a toolbox at my place ... He just knew I had things that needed repairing. He, also, brought champagne and dates ... (the eating kind ... of course ...) on a day cruise.

3. My car broke down ... and I had to lecture out of state. One gentleman drove me ... and waited

outside in the car for one and a half hours ...
(wouldn't let him hear me).

4. Several ... gave me contacts for my career.

5. When I broke up with my beau ... we were still
   good friends. He not only helped me with projects
   ... but let me use his office constantly. One day ...
   had a party ... (he wasn't invited) ... in the
   <u>pouring</u> rain ... he came and fixed my doorbell.

Many ... many ... more.

It's wonderful to know ... all I do is call ... and they're there.

Treat a man like a man ... and you'll get great treats.

That's true for the women ... too!

Men/women of merit always like those who are worth their
attention.

Open your wings and fly with the wind ... or against the
wind ... not wild ... but soaring.

Take a chance ... or chances are ... they will be taken by
somcone else.

And it's so easy to take someone else's ... instead of
<u>developing</u> <u>your</u> <u>own</u>! How negative!

And be in the picture yourself ... not hanging around others
... hoping.

Be proof-positive.

One summer ... not too long ago ... I went to a gabsy gala for singles. Everyone was showered in grand style. There wasn't one ... that didn't have a tip-top time.

But one thing I will never understand ... Why oh why ... do dozens and dozens of gals come together ... group around each other all evening ... or communicate ... with common chit-chat?

Fellows, too!

They're the ones who constantly complain ... *I didn't meet anyone. ... There was no one there. All the good ones were taken.*

Not me! There were four men together ... bingo! Contacts and chuckles were coined.

Then later on ... to three others standing ... just "waiting" for me to join them. They introduced me to a few others. One distinguished gentleman ... exclaimed ... *I want her at my Christmas party. ... I want her at my Christmas party.*

Make contact right away ... Don't lose the opportunity. Seize the occasion ... now!

Samples:

1. Before you attend an affair ... (if you don't
   already have one) ... form a venture or project ...
   for charity ... professional ... singles' trip/dance ...
   a party of your own ... or ... whatever.
   Pass out flyers ... calling cards ... or verbally
   broadcast the event ... so the special one or ones
   you meet ... will be involved.

2. They're going to leave ... run after them ... and
say ... *I forgot something.*
Kiss her/him ... then quickly run back. Don't
allow them to forget you.

Scores of women say ... *Why don't you share the wealth?*

A number of times ... I did! Never ... never ... never ... again.

One acquaintance ... through me ... met a fellow ... who
picked her up at her home in a limousine ... (the neighbors
were impressed) ... and had lunch at the Ritz. The date
didn't work out ... and she had the nerve to say to me ... *You
told him not to call me again* ... Dumb ... dumb ... dumb!

So many more instances ... where they blame me ... instead
of themselves. No wonder ... they never had "luck" on their
own ... they rely on someone else.

Do your own romancing! If you have to lose weight ... study
for an exam/assignment ... go to work ... who does it for you?
Hmmmmm?

Anyhow ... dates are for the pits ... pitted ... no seed ... core ...
or growth.

Bachelors ... believe it or not ... go slow ... at revealing ...
themselves ... and I don't mean ... full monty. Their traits ...
position ... personality.

To catch him ... or her ... you must catch on and care ... listen
... listen ... listen!

One friend was relating the trouble she was having with
her relationship. She told me everything ... except his name
... address ... work (never met him).

I sketched for her ... what his actions would be. Well ... he did exactly what I predicted. She was at a loss ... and upset ... and thought ... somehow I found out his name and address and told him what to do!

Another one!! You figure it out ... I can't be bothered. How did I sense the result of the relationship? Because she related what he said and did. I listened ... listened ... listened ... and understood and realized his features.

Parley not only pleases the palate ... but each other's personality and perception ... Otherwise there is no "play" ... no drama ... no comedy ... no provocation.

You'll be cool ... if you remember ... conversation about the weather is cold fish ... and politics ... hot pepper.

Men/women with character ... (the only kind) ... no matter what position in life ... want and need ... popular ... impressive ... inspirational ... faithful friends. Personally or professionally ... you must keep up.

Be independent. There's nothing wrong ... if ... in a marriage or relationship you take the lead ... sometimes ... (it's a partnership).

Most women ... truly believe the men should go after them ... especially ... the man of their dreams ... on a white horse. Dream on!

Merriment ... molding ... making ... are main factors in l'affaire d'amour. Otherwise ... you're on a merry-go-round!

Act ... action ... activity ... actuate!

Asked <u>over</u> <u>500</u> women ... (20 years and up) ... single/married ...

'What kind of man do you want?'

<u>100%</u> ... <u>without</u> <u>exception</u> ... gave me the <u>expected</u> answers.

Kind ... considerate ... fun ... doesn't drink too much ... has means ... honest ... trustworthy ... likes children ... does things together ... takes care of me ... etc. ... etc. ... etc. ...

<u>Not</u> <u>one</u> ... gave an unusual or creative response.

<u>No</u> <u>one</u> stated ... The kind who I can make giggle ... make <u>him</u> feel wanted ... discover who <u>he</u> is ... <u>his</u> needs ... care for <u>him</u> ...

<u>No</u> <u>one</u> ... <u>except</u> ... oh ... go on ... <u>guess</u>!!!

Men also flirt with the same notions ... or almost the same ...

There are two tragedies in life. One is not to get your heart's desire. The other is to get it.
— George Bernard Shaw

He used to be fairly indecisive, but now he's not so certain.
— Peter Alliss

You may not want to be a star ... or a significant someone ... sometimes a supporting role can be extremely effective ... just <u>be</u> ... and stretch yourself to be the best!

You're not to be led down the garden path ... You're on a superhighway ... jetting or soaring to your destination to show them you're a stand<u>out</u> ... and not a stand-<u>in</u>!

Where is she at the moment? Alone with probably the most attractive man she's ever met. Don't tell me that doesn't beat hell out of hair curlers and late late show.
—Neil Simon

If you're alone ... guaranteed ... you'll find others who are, too!

Start something!

I was going to be alone ... one Christmas eve.

My friend ... who had a bed and breakfast near my church ... let me use his <u>elegant</u> dining room and kitchen ... for free.

I called ... and with the help of another friend and his steady ... gathered a sizable group for a festive holiday dinner ... (<u>more</u> <u>men</u> than women) ... and then most of us went to church.

Why hold back or sit tight? Produce a party tonight.

There <u>never</u> has to be a reason!

My beau at that time ... and I gave a game party at a club ... playing ... mystery ... chess ... cards ...

The waiters were always pleasant to me ... but that evening they were extra special.

'My friend spoke to them.'

My beau thought it was my imagination.

That friend was one of the dearest men I knew ... and president of this club ... at the time.

I asked him ... 'Did you speak to the waiters?'

He answered ... *Yes ... I told them ... I don't want to hear from Lorraine.*

I <u>would</u> have cried to him ... if things weren't right.

But don't you ... unless you have the know-how!

Tears are not the mark of weakness but of power.
—Washington Irving

Laugh and the world laughs with you, weep and you weep alone.
—Ella Wheeler Wilcox

If you would have me weep, you must feel grief yourself.
—Horace

If you overflow ... or fake it ... you know what would happen. Yes ... everyone has ...

Glum drops.
—Anonymous

Whine and pine
or
Wine and dine

And never ...

He is not only dull in himself, but the cause of dullness in others.
—Samuel Foote

If you spent time on your spark ... being sparkling ... you'd be too involved to grumble!! Be grateful ... you're <u>you</u>!

You can do "it" with anyone ... but first develop a dynamic, dramatic persona within you!

No time for stewing ... your soup is on ...

Bowl them over.

It's up to you ... to make your "weak" days ... into sundaes.

Add your own toppings ... subtract your moaning ... multiply your aspirations.

And giggle ... giggle ... giggle ...

Because giggling is just as stirring and seductive as being sexy!

Anyone who laughs at this ... ignore.

<u>Guaranteed</u> ... gigglers got "it"!

Because ....

Your salad days are over.

Chapter II

YOUR SALAD DAYS ARE OVER ...
WHEN YOU POUR ON THE DRESSING

Whatever you do, kid, always serve it with a little dressing.

—Attributed to George M. Cohan

I believe l'amour is an art form ... and a business.

Oh, stop screeching ... <u>not</u> the oldest profession. It's your business to <u>do</u> ... now! "It" sells cars ... films ... clothes ... magazines ... most everything.

Everyone has "it" ... No exceptions.

Being beautiful or handsome is a billion dollar business. Sure ... you were told by others or yourself ... to lose weight ... color or cut your hair ... wear more makeup ... colorful clothes ... etc.

<u>Anyone</u> ... can don a flashy tie or dress ... or be proper in their professional attire.

You may be a puff pastry ... but who <u>ever</u> dines on the <u>outer crust</u> ... <u>alone</u>?

In phyllo dough boereg ... it's the mouth-watering melted cheese that counts. The well-seasoned Beef Wellington ... even by itself ... that is the winner. Sweetened, juicy apples ... give the pie star appeal.

In other woids ... your inner practice and principles are poignant.

Okay ... you've heard this before ... but you still swallow that the young ... good-looking ... shapely ... are the only ones who can be hot stuff!

Ha!

Stop being the cat's paw ... Start being the cat's meow ... and purrrrr!

Any resemblance to my being young ... good looking ... shapely ... is ridiculous.

Howevvvvver ... enthralling ... enchanting ... unequaled ... yes!

Come on board! Sail to uncharted ports ... changing currents ... amazing adventures ... Cruise and choose your own course in your own backyard.

Notice your full-length portrait instead of a snapshot. But remember ...

Genius is one percent inspiration and ninety-nine percent perspiration.
—Thomas Edison

Do you suppose ... Cindy Crawford ... Cher ... Oprah ... George Hamilton ... Regis Philbin ... Richard Gere ... were born with that certain something?

All notable people puzzle out their personage ... their goals ... then practice ... practice ... practice. Anyone who has achieved ... did it through effort.

Secure is sexy ... not ... ché sera sera. Otherwise ... you're flat ... out of tune ... and stuck on one chord ... instead of playing a concerto.

Some ... would rather waffle with a liaison ... fudge around with their feelings ... or have their cake and eat it ... too ... without any frosting!

No matter what sex ... It's smart to be square ... but not a square. By the way ... no triangles ... the percussions can be resounding.

It's not only Victor's secret ... and yes, Virginia, you, too ...

There is a decent ... terrific one with values ... waiting for you.

Go ... go ... go ... and he/she ... will go for you.

Develop and discover what's around the corner ... and aspire to be the new kid on the block ... no matter what age!

Variety is the spice of life.
—William Cowper

Be ready ... to sprout in stages ... as though you were on stage. The mirror is your audience.

How to be ... how not to be ... no questions ... answers!

But never ... never ... never ... too hard or severe in any of these exercises or workouts ...

And never ... if you have medical or physical problems. Always consult your physician.

There are several recipes ... here are some spoonfuls.

A WINK WORKS WONDERS

When you wink ... you must smile.

And when you smile ... your eyes will automatically twinkle. Try it!

Awwwww ... go on ... I'm not ordering ... but urging you.

A woman attorney is so grateful I taught her this. *It does work wonders.*

Events that were bitter or biting may become a bit more mediocre. A wonderful ... warm way in any situation. Repeat it often.

It helps relieve your tension and theirs. It could make them trust you more ... and yourself.

If you want to give happiness ... wink.

I can take care of that
Don't worry ...
Everything is going to be all right.
Gishee-gishee ... goo! Isn't that (my) babykins cute?

Weddings ... funerals ... meetings ... hospitals ... no matter where you are.

If you think I mean wink ... to nab a married man ... a pickup ... a sordid affair ... the boss for a raise ... or to employees ... you might as well toss this book away ... and leave!

I've winked for years ... and <u>no</u> <u>one</u> <u>ever</u> took me the wrong way. Why? Because people see who I am tout de suite ... My actions tell all.

As a motivational speaker ... I spoke to a group ... <u>all</u> <u>men</u> ... (some were international businessmen) ... and disclosed their Herculean attributes ... as well as their Achilles' heels.

I didn't pull any punches. There was absolutely ... positively ... <u>no</u> ... <u>not</u> <u>a</u> <u>speck</u> ... of chauvinistic attitude or overtures. We respected each other. It was wonderful.

The one who engaged me ... called two days later ... and stated ... the men thought I was a hit. He booked me for a national convention.

At a Rotary club event ... the president disclosed to all ... that they have a speaker once a week ... and no one ever received a standing ovation. One guess ... who they gave one to!

Yes ... they winked. It does work wonders.

If you encourage them to wink back ... they will gladly do so ... and <u>most</u> of the time ... <u>giggle</u>!

<u>Original</u> <u>Whoopee</u> <u>Workouts</u>

Gotcha!

Like a cold bath. You think it does you good because you feel better when you stop it.

—Robert Quiller

Not mine! These feats are full of fun and fanfare. Lose weight on your own time. This time ... it's mind over matter ... to spur you on and help you realize you can have spirit ... strength ... and sex appeal.

These exercises will hopefully make you do the unexpected.

Practice ... practice ... practice ... being poised and take pride in yourself ... before you plunge in.

The rule is ... there are no rules ... Do what you want ... but make sure you know what you're doing ... and to spoil someone's stock ... you could be in the soup ... stewing! Vicious vichyssoise is venerable.

Roll out your barrel ... filled with super-duper surprises ... a show-off? Yes! Why camouflage? You'll catch on ... that by being carefree ... you will care for others.

Women are known for their instinct ... but men are keen on body language. They can instantly tell whether you're ... a hot tamale ... soft/hard-boiled ... over easy ... well cooked ... a cold fish ... a juicy plum ... a rotten tomato ... a cool cucumber.

And women should suspect or be savvy that at first ... or even later ... maybe it's the crust they are being courted with ... not his ginger ... garlic ... pepper personality.

These aren't the only flavorings ... There are so many right recipes ... It's up to you ... to take stock and study the cookbooks out there ...

Take yourself off the shelf ... Simmer slowly. Don't skim ... but be cultured ... whether you're serious ... silly ... smooth or sharp.

Your <u>stance</u> will attract ... because it is saying ... *I'm somebody ... are you?* You'd be amazed ... how they are itching to prove it.

Movie stars of today ... but <u>especially</u> those of the '20s and '30s ... were privy as to how to pour on the dressing ... and how!!! Spicy ... sappy ... succulent! Pour over these crème de la crème celebrities.

Mae West ... Garbo ... Humphrey Bogart ... Gary Cooper ... and others ... never jiggle or jerk like jello! Cary Grant ... James Cagney ... Clara Bow ... Jean Harlow ... may jaunt ... but are silky ... symmetrical ... satiny with a crash of symbols.

You, too ... can make music ... with a touch of mystery.

Don't say ... *No!* ... but ... *I ... I ... I ... I ... I ... I ...*

Then the ayes will have "it" ... which may soon become <u>we</u> ... mais qui.

Music hath charms to sooth a savage breast.
                                        —Congreve

The only language in which you cannot say a mean or sarcastic thing.
                                        —John Erskine

If you let music inspire and encourage you, you can be a beauty ... not a beaut! Handsome ... not some old hand.

Tunes ... classical ... dance ... folk ... country ... foreign ... swing ... rock 'n' roll ... try them all ... it will bring out personalities and traits you never knew you had. You will understand how to charm ... capture ... conquer.

Music will help you to have winning ways ... and your eyes will be as bright as Rudolph's nose ... but not as red.

As a woman ... you should be the dancer ... prancer ... and romancer ... so men will dash away ... dash away ... all to you!

As a man ... you won't be so frosty ... Let your snow melt and be merry ... and every day be a holiday.

Let's relate without words. Well-read body language can be useful ... and others won't "use" you.

Mesmerize with your eyes ... You don't have to be <u>bad</u> ... to be <u>"good"</u>!

Practice with pantomime with any ... peaceful ... slowwwwwer than molasses ... music ... a <u>must</u>!

Look into the mirror ... Let it talk back to you ... and be fault-finding ... There will come a time ... when you won't have to ask ... who is the fairest ... You'll tell that image ... 'I'm not fair ... I'm paramount!'

But for now ... on with the music ...

Stand ... straight ... solid ... steady ... head upright ... eyes bright ... hands down at side ... now ... <u>very</u> ... <u>very</u> ... <u>very</u> ...

<u>very</u> ... slowly ... <u>inch</u> <u>by</u> <u>inch</u> ... move your hands ... and arms to your hips.

<u>Never</u> ... <u>ever</u> with your <u>palms</u> <u>up</u> ... palms up is not only unrefined ... but shows insecurity.

Let's go on ...

At this point ... flutter your finger<u>tips</u> <u>only</u>. Fingertips are wonderful exercises ... because if you stretch them as far as you can ... (as in life) ... you will feel a slight sensation in doing so.

Remember ... nothing else moves ... I <u>know</u> you have to blink! <u>Discipline</u> ... <u>Development</u> ... <u>Direction</u>!

Continue now with hands and arms ... with fingertips still fluttering ... up to your chest ... then eye level. Waaaaave ... to and fro ... your fingertips and hands from left to right ... eyes following movements.

Still ... at a <u>snail's pace</u> ... (This is <u>so</u> important) ... raise your hands and arms above your head ... extend your fingers ... as far as they will reeeach! And hold.

Nooooo! You are not going to break!

With the same speed ... slooooowly ... inch by inch ... bring your hands and arms down to your side and hold.

Now give out a gigantic sigh. Repeat and repeat. The <u>exercise</u> ... the <u>exercise</u>!

Oh ... you're not used to this ... It's too difficult ... (Not!) ... Who needs it? ... <u>Everyone</u>!!!

It's sooooo easy to flit and be frisky ... in this jet and juicy age. In our liaisons ... work ... travel ... cooking ... correspondence ... dancing ... emotions ... etc. ... we've been spoiled to be speedy. By being quick ... we forget or miss being quiet ...

Though most of my friends will swear to you ... I'm never silent. Yes ... I do breeze along in my actions and words. But I realize that men like to talk ... once in a while ... especially ... when dozens say ...

Will you let me get a word in edgewise ...
Will you listen to me?
Now it's my turn to do the talking.

Notice ... they don't leave ... and I <u>do</u> listen.

Men always give you a green light ... or a warning signal. Read their signs ...

Men be mindful, too!

Both ... It goes back to <u>you</u>.

Silent and smooth are always appealing.

Practice ... to hold that placid ... peaceful poise. Remember to relax.

When you elaborate ... the workout will become entertaining ... enjoyable and winning. The training and tune ... soon ... will appear natural to you.

Stand without moving or being stiff ... it will give you confidence and be convincing to others. Your body will be unbent and your impressions and expressions ... hopefully will be on target ... and hit the mark ... every time.

When you're assured that you've achieved that area ... when you can stand erect without moving a muscle ... you are on your way to being sturdy and not susceptible.

Everyday occurrences that can be annoying ... could be amusing.

Picture this ... standing perfectly still ... head high ... mouth closed and eyes not flinching ... others ... are in awe of you.

This manner can be productive to a nasty co-worker ... a snippy "friend" ... any ticket office ... crowded subway ... returning an item ...

If ... if ... if ... you rehearse ... rehearse ... rehearse ... ahead of time ... you will cut the mustard.

You'll come out ahead ... even if they're thundering ... sarcastic or sickening sweet with a smug smile.

A movement ... such as a twitching of the head ... neck ... hand ... shifting ... looking down or sideways ... (instead of straight towards them) ... no matter how slight ... sends a signal ... you've not only abandoned yourself ... but your audience.

Secure ... steadfast ... scores a success.

When <u>that</u> technique is triumphant ... onto the next ... to be loose and limber.

Ever notice the ones that flaunt in a flash

Are always the ones with no polish or panache?

So many flit or flirt without feeling.

Who do you <u>think</u> you are ... taking the lead ... without creating your character ... studying your lines ... blocking the scenes out ... and having "petty" tryouts?

A few years ago ... I taught artistry at four skating clubs. If you're aware of the judging ... it's 50% artistry ... and 50% technique.

I noticed that numerous skaters were talented at technique ... but had no clue how to emote with the choreography ... music ... judges ... or the spectators. Several ballet dancers ... gymnasts ... singers and models ... the same ... Coached them, too!

Anna Pavlova and Beverly Sills were known for their <u>great acting</u> ... not just their dancing and singing.

One club believed that the skater ... they wanted me to teach ... could be a champion ... (which she was) ... but didn't sparkle ... no facial expressions.

She looked like a classic ballerina with delicate features and physique; and at first ... thought my lessons ... bizarre and far-out.

You will ... too ... but they can be fun and full of fervor and help give you a boost with bounce.

Ohhhhh ... You're not aggressive ... affected ... animated.

This above all: to thine own self be true,
And it must follow, as the night the day,

Thou canst not then be false to any man.
　　　　　　　　　　　　—Shakespeare

Particularly to yourself.

It's up to you ... to spring forward and jump out of the cake ... or sit there and drink sours ... wondering why others succeed.

Onward!

Stand still in front of a full-length mirror. It still might imagine you're a drip ... with these workouts ... but just wink ... and say ... *Someday ... I'm going to be a big splash!*

Remember ... body completely motionless. Widen ... stretch ... and roll your eyes ... overdo ... but <u>not</u> too hard.

<u>Then</u> ... make <u>wild</u> ... <u>zany</u> ... facial expressions ... especially with your mouth ... Frown ... smirk ... show your teeth ... curl your lips ... move them from side to side ... up and down ... around and around ... <u>Loosen</u> up all your facial muscles and be <u>foolish</u> while doing it.

Learn ... laugh ... be ludicrous.

You may shake your hands ... Put your shoulders up and down ... Wiggle your derriere ... then bump and grind your entire body ... without moving your feet!

Sleek ... swinging ... not skittish or self-conscious.

Now ... go for it ... Flow forward and backward ... up and down ... Move <u>everything</u> ... including your emotions ... like a moppet! Yes ... men can be moppets ... too!

Select music that is spry ... and gives you the mood. The best pieces are children's ditties ... light ... limber ... lovable.

Foolish faces ... and a flexible frame ... does not create a clown ... but a captivating chou-chou ... that is glowing ... graceful ... elegant ... cultivated ... suave.

Why? Because when you give a performance in public ... (we're always in an act ... somewhere ... somehow) ... you sense when to be silent ... suspenseful ... swinging ... steadfast ... suasive ... sensitive ... bouncy ... and smooth as butter.

It was fruitful for the skaters ... dancers ... professionals ... and others ... It can be peachy for you.

You'll uncover a side of you that has been sleeping. Recognize ... no one is perfect ... and no one minds the thorns in a full-bloom rose ...

Nip it in the bud ... and that bud will never wilt ... or be weak ... but will grow and burst forth.

If you whine ... you can't win.

Your past is passé. You can't be passionate if you're passive. Soon ... your passport could be stamped ... sexy.

Sex does come before sexy ... but <u>only</u> when it is alphabetized in the dictionary ... not in an affair of the heart.

Warm up your buns ... before you become a tropical heat wave. Then you can achieve cakes and ales as a cool ... colorful cocktail.

This isn't checkers ... where you quickly jump over a man/woman ... to win ... or a fast card game of fish ... where you hook it in five minutes.

Compare your achievements and relationships to bridge ... where it takes time and effort to comprehend the theories. How you and your partner should match conventions ... and acquire the same footing.

Then you won't have to kick each other underneath the table ... to send signals.

Your bidding ... finesses ... and slams ... should be a smash.

Whether you're fuming or flirting ... your flashing eyes ... fancy-free spirit ... can express more ... than fast or feigned foreplay.

There can be no debate or dispute ... if you take a <u>stand</u>. Sometimes silence can have its golden moments.

Of course ... a few <u>coined</u> words ... can gild the lily ...

The opera ain't over 'til the fat lady sings.
—Dan Cook

And ...

The game isn't over ... until the referee knows how to blow his/her whistle.

Virgin Exercises for the Voice

Anything ... to grab your attention.

A vigorous voice is vital.

Did you realize Clark Gable cultivated his voice to be robust ... rugged and refined?

A voice must be velvety ... voluptuous ... vivacious ... for you to be visible ... and uncover your ....

Valuable visage.

Voice ... don't varnish!

The organ of the soul.

—Longfellow

I don't want to talk grammar. I want to talk like a lady.

—George Bernard Shaw

Language most shews a man; speak, that I may see thee.

—Ben Jonson

If you're lovable ... you're able to do anything.

With vogue and variety ... not being vapid and vague.

Pack a punch with pizzazz. Notice how a powerful ... polished voice can be persuasive and provocative.

Dozens of times ... I made screaming babies stop ... on the spot ... just by my spunky ... suasive sound ... "Stop!"

Some mothers thanked me ... others stared with their mouths open ... and all wondered ... how on earth ... did I do that?

With tip-top ... tints and tones.

Now pretty pleeeeese!

Open your mouth like an orange ... and say ... Ohhhhh ... for pear-shaped tones ... spongy and striking ... not grapes or prunes ... shriveled and dried up.

By being frost-free ... filled with flavorings ... you can't fail.

And lower ... lower ... looooowerrrrr ... your timbre ...

Notice any celebrity or public figure ... their quality is low ... firm ... and impressive ... not waaaaay ... uppppp ... here ... or teensy-weensy ... sheepish ... or sugar-coated.

Are you flashing back ...

I'm just an ordinary guy/gal.
I'm not or don't want to be famous.
What do I care what they do?
Natural is okay for me.

Natural is nuts! <u>Naturally</u> is numero uno.

No one is asking you to be famous ... (though you can ... if you fancy it).

But to add frosting to your cake ... rather than leftover crumbs ...

You, too, can be a <u>forget</u>-<u>me</u>-<u>not</u> ... instead of crabgrass.

If you only recognize and respect what sterling and striking sounds ... can win one's spurs.

Always require the best ... of a relationship ... your friends ... your career ...

In a restaurant ... correct billing ... car repairs ... travel ... telephone service ... or whatever.

One time ... a telephone repairman came to my home ... and stated ... *I hear you're having trouble with your phone lines.*

My response ... 'I'm not having trouble ... <u>you</u> are.'

You're right.

We both <u>giggled</u> ... I told him he looked like Mel Gibson ... (meant it) ... we giggled some more ... and he did a terrific job.

Naturally!

<u>Numerous</u> times ... I've stopped gentlemen at the airport ... no matter what age ...

'Would you carry my heavy bags? ... I'll tip you.'

Not <u>one</u> <u>time</u> ... <u>ever</u> ...

1. Did they refuse me
2. "Carry off" my luggage
3. Want the gratuity

Once in a <u>great</u> while ... when there is <u>no</u> <u>other</u> route ... to accomplish or negotiate my objective ... I'd speak out ...

'You don't want me to raise the roof ... do you?'

<u>Always</u> ... the answer is *No!*

However ... a sentimental serene silence ... can be like a golden apple ... <u>delicious</u>! A juicy apple a day ... helps keep your mate from straying away.

But ... one also must cook up ...

<u>Apple</u>: ... dumplings ... sauce ... baked ... crumb cake ... deep dish ... stuffing ... fritters ... and spiced ... Omit ... pickled and crab.

Don't label yourself.

He knew the precise psychological moment when to say nothing.
—Oscar Wilde

Women, too!

And ...

Oh, fie, Miss, you must not kiss and tell.
—Congreve

"They are fools who kiss and tell"—
Wisely has the poet sung
Man may hold all sorts of posts
If he'll only hold his tongue
                              —Kipling

Even when you're steaming ... the voice is never choppy or coarse ... but always colorful.

Absolutely not ... dry as toast ... dull ... mechanical ... monotonous!

That cursory ... cockish phrase ... *Have a nice day* Should be dropped like a disastrous soufflé.

Your sounds should go <u>up</u> ... at the end of every sentence.

Most ... go <u>down</u>! Notice news anchors and panelists on TV.

<u>Up</u> ... is always better!!

To <u>lower</u> your tones ... say ahhhhh ... several times.

Not only ... ahhhhh ... but ahh /^\ sigh ... /^\ sigh aaah ... /^\ sigh ahhh ... aaaaaaah!

Feel and say it lower ... (yummy in your tummy) ... but utter it ... <u>uppity up</u> ... not downtrodden.

If at first you don't succeed, try, try again. Then quit. No use being a damn fool about it.
                              —W.C. Fields

You'll be pound foolish ... full of sour grapes ... and red herrings ... if you follow that flow.

Everyone enjoys singing. Oh, ... some of you don't. Well ... sing anyway.

You don't want to ... and don't dig being told what to do. Good! ... You're on your way ... <u>but</u> ... you're not <u>there</u> ... <u>yet</u>!!!

Take away that pudding — it has no theme.
                              —Winston Churchill

Or rather:

His smile bathed us like warm custard.
                              —Basil Boothroyd

A silly song will smooth and soften your speech.

My original lyrics can be laughable ... if you whoop it up.

Men, this is for you ... too! Just add your own ingredients!

All ... dip into the lyrics with honey ... and <u>ham</u> "it" up!

"I'm Ready"

by Lorraine

Here I am content as can be.

I have my man guessing about me.

Here's the clue: act bored as can be—and
Have him think you will
Always be ready!

Refrain:

I don't need you ... I've never needed you ... but if you need love ...

I'm ready.

I don't want you ... I never wanted you ... but if you want (sigh) ...

I'm ready.

I'm only good for making you happy ...

You like me best when I am snappy.

So if you adore me ... charm me ... don't bore me ...

I'm ready ...

I don't find you ... I never want to find you ... but if you find me ...

I'm ready ...

I don't have to ... I never had to ... but if you (sigh) ...

I'm ready.

I always put on a comfortable smock ...

When I hear you using my key in the lock.

When I'm on a divan ... I know that I can ...

Be ready.

Enunciate with expression.

At first ... you should vant to be alone ... with just your mirror and merriment ... Then when you're ready ... wow!!!

Wear Yourself Out

What did Marilyn Monroe wear to bed ...

Chanel No. 5.

A bun with a pun.

Most of us ... are not cutouts of Monroe. But we can certainly mold and shape ourselves into a buffet or in the buff ... with only an apron on ... full-length ... if you're bad at the knees ... and only with your sweetie pie.

It isn't what you wear ... but how you wear it out.

Formal ... or informal ... it depends which course you are serving.

By now ... you should be convincing when you stand still. Notice ... not only will your body become straightforward ... but your feelings should be secure and not be susceptible.

And what a dynamic ... decisive voice can accomplish ...

But only if ... you achieve those areas ... then you're on the yellow brick road to find the bluebird of happiness.

O, how bitter a thing it is to look into happiness through another man's eyes.

—Shakespeare

Oh, make us happy and you make us good.

—R. Browning

And how! Your voice and your posture aren't the only things you'll uncover that can be potent!

Vantage ... venture ... variety ... vivacity ... <u>vogue</u>!

If you are not in fashion, you are nobody.

—Lord Chesterfield

She wears her clothes as if they were thrown on with a pitchfork.

—Jonathan Swift

When he buys his ties, he has to ask if gin will make them run.

—F. Scott Fitzgerald

Since Adam and Eve ... the craze for clothes has always been consequential and critical ... in more ways ... than you can count.

You believe not? Then why ...

1. Don't you wear your birthday suit ... constantly? Hmmmmm?
2. Attending any event ... formal ... sports ... soirée ... you ask ... *What are you wearing?*

Both men/women question all the time. Even,
me!
3. School ... career ... social ... ad ... dress ... ing the
public ... etc. ... You're conscious how you cook ...
er look.

Day in ... day out ... have a code in dress. No matter how
offhand the affair ... offhand ... not offhanded.

The selections you were shown ... were stillness ...
stretching ... swaying ...

Now ... you should feel like floating and flirting with flair.
With the aid of fashion ... You could be spicy, smooth ...
samba ... or swinging.

Take off those clogs ... heavy sneakers ... or lumberjack
boots.

Take off those skintight ... baggy ... fuddy-duddy ... corny ...
far-out ... or way-out habits.

Your outfit ... should <u>fit</u> <u>out</u> ... you and the occasion ... not
with ordinary fads. Swim with your own style.

Look and act like no one else ... Why hop on another's
bandwagon ... unless ... <u>their</u> concord jets.

Break the sound barrier, and trip and fall for the light
fantastic! Just fling your fancies.

Flashy ... without flaunting ... frivolous without being a
fool.

Fashion will facilitate your frostings.

Mysterious ... musical ... merry ... memorable!

Don't allow anyone ... anywhere ... anytime ... to forget who you are.

Dive in with your own tidal wave.

No more slow boats ... <u>show</u> boats ... because you're not a yawl ... but a yacht!

Whoop it up ... before whoopee ...
A loving lullaby before beddy-bye.

In other woids ... pour on the <u>dressing</u> ... before you serve the salad.

The feedback?

An appealing appetizer ... elegant entrées and desirable desserts.

If you have designs ... on someone at any stage ... you don't have to be ... suave ... swanky ... or snazzy ... just spirited ... social ... and stylish.

A while back ... I suspected I was <u>so</u> smart ... that I wore a bright blonde wig ... and gold dress to symphony! Jamais ... jamais ... encore.

That was years ago ... when <u>window</u> <u>dressing</u> ... <u>suited</u> me more than a roll ... with seasonings and sesame seeds.

Today ... most swallow that Windows ... on the Internet ... gathering <u>material</u> and <u>designs</u> ... is better connected than actuating material and designs tete-a-tete!

If only those mechanisms ... would tilt ... so we could tilt ... more together ... instead of machines being matchmaker to anything and everything we do.

Though it's clear ... they are ... a certainty.

A place for everything and everything in its place.

—Isabella Beeton

The machine may be ... piquant ... and provide you with provisions. You can hug it ... tie a huge red ribbon around it ... and it can get under your skin ... but <u>it</u> still doesn't have "it."

You can't softly squeeze that gismo ... and ... make goo-goo eyes or bill and coo ... while doing a belly dance.

Actually ... hundreds ... at gatherings ... act like they are mingling with mechanical devices ... or they themselves ... are too technical.

A couturier is distingué
But at any soirée
You, too, can display
If you portray your own panaché.

You are what you <u>wear</u> ... <u>anywhere</u>!

Do you remember that gabsy gala ... ? <u>Most</u> all the gals wore the "traditional" headdress of the twenties.

<u>One</u> ... person wore a white satin <u>hat</u> ... Garbo style ('20s) ... with regal rhinestones around the band. Three men ... stopped her to comment ... she was hip and a hit. One man

... a month later ... at another gathering ... reminded her of the chapeau.

Awwwww ... you knew all along ... who wore that headdress.

I could don a $4.00 hat to the market ... bridge ... shopping ... and strangers or friends ... but <u>especially</u> men ... would stop me ... and comment on my hat.

A girlfriend ... couldn't find me at a tennis match ... She told the usher ... *She always wears a hat* ......

Not always!

One time ... my steady friend argued with me for several minutes ... in a department store ... when I told him to buy a certain chapeau ... for himself. He knew I was going to win ... (He wasn't used to that) ... and bought it.

He wore it out ... The hat! The hat!

Chapeau has an aura ... a mystique. Sport many novel and special hats ... but not ... with your hat in your hand ...

Fashion should be fun ... because you are.

It isn't <u>what</u> you <u>wear</u> ... <u>but</u> <u>how</u> <u>you</u> <u>wear</u> <u>it</u> <u>out</u>!!!

What seems to be worn out with many is ... <u>manners</u>!

Market Your Manners

There should be a method in your manners.

You don't have to be a lord and lady ... Then again ... you <u>are</u> a lord and lady ...

No matter what station you're in ... we all can be trained to arrive at the same stop ... at being respectful of others.

If you're nice as pie
You're the apple of everyone's eye.

Politeness is an easy virtue, and has great purchasing power.
> —A.B. Alcott

He is the very pineapple of politeness!

> —Richard Sheridan

All my friends <u>are</u>. Otherwise ... they don't exist!

And whoever declared one shouldn't ask about their ... family ... friends ... dreams ... hobbies ... work ... traditions ... heritage ... is <u>not</u> successful in the singles scene ... and is wet or dry behind the ears.

<u>Go</u> <u>for</u> <u>it</u> ... right away ... There rarely is a next time.

So <u>many</u> have wailed ...

   1. *Wish I had spoken up.*

2. *Why didn't I ask for their number?*
3. *When will I see him/her again?*
4. *Gee ... I wonder if I made a mistake ... not knowing him/her better?*

Yes ... you did!!

To hesitate is human ... to ask divine ...
To find out about a Carl or Caroline

Plow right in and discover the dirt ... or the flowering plants.

That ugly duckling may be a <u>swan</u> or that gander ... just a <u>silly</u> goose!

Make out ... before you make out.

Your interest ... is always inviting ... particularly ... if you use your imagination in inquiring ... they'll imagine you important.

<u>Care</u> ... but not <u>crude</u>.

If they have tip-top traits ... <u>tell</u> them ... It'll radiate not only their colors ... but your own.

When you're in the know
You'll know when to say ... whoaaaaa!

And trot away.

If they don't come up to your standards ... or they are <u>way</u> above yours ...

Get with it ... or out of it.

When I first met a very close friend ... I couldn't care less.

Was chairman of a boat party for a candidate running for governor ... (did so ... to meet men) ... and this special man was on my team.

We both admitted ... if we weren't working as a group ... we would not ever have been close.

He was an entrepreneur ... and a true ... masculine gentleman ... but not a natty dresser.

He became chic ... nifty ... and more charming.

I became calmer ... tactful (somewhat) ... and cosmopolitan.

And much more.

How? We learned and laughed together ... with consideration and courtesy ... <u>court</u>esy ...

Thank yous are tasty ... mais merci beaucoup est delicieux.

If your manner is mannerly ... and you've <u>marketed</u> <u>your</u> <u>manners</u> ...

You've now advanced to be ....

An ambrosial appetizer!

Chapter III

"HOT" HORS D'OEUVRES

Why do you want to "make" them?

Because:

You're in high spirits.
Beating your bitterness.
Letting off steam.
Preserving your poulet.
Stirring new-fashioned friends.
Having a bunch of blues.
Pouring on the gravy for a particular party.
A fruitful/flop in business.

Replace your rehashed "recipes" ... and rise up to a rare you ... that will be home on the range. "Hot" hors d'oeuvres is a cool first course to whet the appetite.

It's a stock trend today, to be ... salty and snappy ... peppered with ideas ... to take a snip here and there and split. This causes not just a storm in a teacup ... but puts you and others in the soup ... with king-sized portions.

You will be a show ... <u>stopper</u>!

Serve up alluring appetizers that others will hunger for. Don't open that door until the bell rings ... and you're bubbly and ready. Don't let anyone <u>peach</u> on you or you on them.

Make Mercury confess and peach
those thieves which he himself did teach.

—Samuel Butler

It's smart to be square ... subtle ... selective ... a cut above others. At the <u>right</u> angles ... you'll always be smooth and straight.

L'amour ... l'amour ... toujours l'amour.
It's evermore or nevermore.

You won't become stale or a stick in the mud; instead ... you're going to shake and "make."

Don't take these pinches with a grain of salt ... or that it's a pie in the sky ... Rather ... smack your lips over a pie that is dripping with juices.

Be a show-off with garnish and seasonings! Not fresh ... but with freshness.

Let's sprout ... with a social gathering that is not only sharp ... but has savoir-faire.

A party is like a play ... and you must play the part. Be a Star ... Producer ... Director ... Playwright ... a Designer ... of fashion ... set ... lighting ... invitations ... and themes ... More will take its course here and in other chapters.

Tallulah Bankhead barged down the Nile last night as Cleopatra ... and sank.
—John Mason Brown

Remember ... Look into your oven too soon ... and your <u>soufflé</u> <u>will</u> sink.

My only regret in the theatre is that I could never sit out front and watch me.

—John Barrymore

A watched pot never boils. No more watching and being the leftovers ... From now on ... you're going to pan for gold.

How many parties ... private or public ... where you had to sift and strain through ... and say ... "Of all the joints" ... I had to walk into this one.

Where they give you a canapé and a napkin, and it doesn't matter which one you put in your mouth ... Both taste the same.

—Lucius Beebe

There's no flip side to ... topics ... traditions ... menu ... manners ... and at most, table talk is corn chips ... pretzels ... or stale chestnuts.

We're going to flip-flop from formal and form to a fun-filled function of our own.

Here's the scoop! Flash!! ... Not quite! But we are going to whip it up.

You, yourself, are going to be the crème de la crème. Make sure you don't <u>ever</u> use sour ... not healthy!

You must thirst ... hunger ... be rarin' to go ... Hot to trot ... and cool ... before you present the pièce de résistance ... <u>you</u> ... and your party.

When you want to be ... or do a special treat ... you should read the recipe over and over ... to be sure <u>the</u> <u>contents</u> <u>are</u> <u>correct</u>.

So what if you're plain ... bland ... or a nerd with curd. Even the most flavorful forms, with just the right seasonings, can sink ... if they serve no surprises.

It isn't what you serve ... but <u>how</u> you serve "it" up! You can be a falling or shooting star ... a big cheese or a never-caught little fish ... It's up to you!

At your own reception ... don't offer <u>only</u> refreshments! Pen ... produce ... and perform with pizzazz!

Wow them with your house specials. Don't skim ... sizzle! Let props chip in and give you that zip ... and mushroom you into being peppery.

Wear a bunch of grapes (seedless) with your somewhat low-cut gown ... Just don't let them peel them too soon.

A black tie with no tie or no jacket ... with a comical apron ... a colorful vest — oh ... yes ... for <u>now</u> ... with trousers!

Toss an orange up and down ... from side to side ... to each other ... just "catch" the effect.

Flip your wig ... with a captivating or comical chapeau or crown ... a mesmeric mask ... fan ... cane ... boa ... chiffon scarf ... a splash minted by you.

Loosen up ... but not loose. Don't serve cheesecake ... raise cane ... or especially turn turtle. But go for it ... because you <u>are</u> "it."

How many times did you greet guests with bushels of pecks ... hugs ... and handshakes ... that were set in a mold! Cheese it!

Duck the routine forms. There are <u>no</u> rules! <u>You</u> ... and <u>only</u> you ... set the flavor and pattern ... Everyone will crisscross over. You now have the crust to start rolling ... with your <u>ing</u>redients.

As they flow through the door ...

The hell with "Hello"!

Seductively ... take off their jacket or coat and toss them an apron.

—You! In the kitchen! Take out the ice!

—Split! (They never do!)

—Goodbye! So sorry you have to leave. (They never do.)

—I didn't invite you!

—Who <u>are</u> you??

—Ohhh ... It's you!

—Ohhhhhhhhhh! ... It's yoooouuuuu!!!

Order ... sugarcoat ... insult ... scallop or carp on their tie or dress ... Cook up funny faces ... more!

Snap them up in your arms and dance ... or rock 'n' roll to your tune.

You'll be in the chips if you chirp ... opera ... currant hits ... children's ditties ... saucy songs ... pop ... your cork with creativity ... here ... there ... everywhere! And everyone will rise to your candied bites ... and swallow it up.

It has <u>always</u> … been peaches and cream for me. <u>Not</u> <u>one</u> time … did I have a rotten banana!

If you find <u>one</u> that doesn't gulp it down … he/she is as dull as dishwater … and it's <u>your</u> failure! You hashed it up by arranging to be shown up … by inviting this squash.

Or if one guest is a snip … saucy … or a trickster … you be the treat.

Don't quiver like jello. Just pour on the milk or whipped cream and say …

<u>Silently</u>!!! …… Fudge to you! I'm a four-<u>star</u> chef … and cut capers with everyone else who came to sow their oats. Shell it out!

It's not the men in my life that counts … It's the life in my men.
—Mae West

When a man knows a woman is a woman.

—Gina Lollobrigida

Stop scraping the bottom of your pan. Take the stuffing out of your stuffiness … and strut your stuff.

Even I was a snob! I was so stewed and squeamish when my mother had her guests help themselves in the kitchen. No one else seemed to be sheepish about it. She was always before her time.

Now I follow that formula. It's fun!

As I said ... It never happened to me ... but if there are lemons ... squeeze them out so they won't spoil the broth ... or sweeten and water them down to lemonade. If they want to be served ... tell them to go ... to a restaurant!

Or you yourself might leap to say to me—

You!
>—*There are many who don't maintain ... that it is manners ... or in the mood to allow guests to pitch in.*

Me! La di dah!

>—They're the minuses ... who are mannequins ... Never on the move to the millennium.

You!
>—*The majority may want to loaf and roost ... rather than buck about.*

Me!
>—Let them eat cake or TV dinners and sleep on the sofa on their own time.

Throw them a fish.

It is to be observed that "angling" is the name given to fishing by people—who can't fish.
>—Stephen Leacock

He loved to walk sideways toward them, like a grimly playful crab.
>—R.C. Robertson Glasgow

A wingding is where we flock together. Jar the jar upside down ... and <u>twist</u> the cover ... What you pour out is pure gravy. Shake the soda ... If it's flat, it fizzles out. If it fizzles, it flows all over!

There are countless concoctions you can curry.

1. Score ... with a shark ... or a friend ... who's savvy on the culinary skills. From scratch ... they steer the students on how to be an extraordinary epicurean. Everyone tosses in their talent ... drop by drop ... to dash off a delectable delicacy.

The discovery of a new dish does more for the happiness of mankind than the discovery of a new star.

—Antheline Brillat-Savarin

Anyone who tells a lie has not a pure heart, and cannot make a good soup.
—Ludwig Van Beethoven

2. Or everybody exposes their exclusive edibles.

Okay ... you duckwickies!

The marvelous thing about a joke with a double meaning is that it can only mean one thing.
—Ronnie Barker

Not tonight, Josephine.
—Napoleon I (R.H. Horne)

When your guests enter with their colorful exotic cuisines ... they can exclaim ... *I did it my way.*

Everyone will be pleased as punch to present their chef d'oeuvre! Not one will mince their words ... or feel like mincemeat.

3. To go a bit hog wild, let them bring their recipes and fixings to your place and mix well together ... to foam a menu.
4. Or you be the connoisseur and create your own spread ... They serve ... clean up ... and <u>clean</u> up.

Fancy a frisky festivity ... that will never be a filmy flat frappe. Where Tom, Dick, Harry ... Ann, Jane, Mary ... can have a whale of a time, when thrown in together ... to help or hinder ... make a mess ... drop things ... dash ... bang ... and boom ... opening cupboards and drawers to find the right dish ... pot or utensil. Bumping into each other ... Being the expert or rotten chef ... Again ... <u>my</u> way ... "Cutely" arguing ... cutting up vegetables ... as well as being a cutup ... slicing ... dicing ... laying it on thick ... Being fresh as a mint and fresh with a tomato! Crack an egg ... and your nail ... Spill the beans ... and spill beet juice on someone's attire ... Gum up the works ... Being sticky about licking someone else's bowl ... Cursing while pounding the ice ... apologizing ... while trying to break the ice with someone you go bananas for.

If you had a recent operation or were in a skiing accident ... don't be a grape jelly or a beaten biscuit ... Pour on the jam ... trim your crust ... and rule the roost at the bar or music area. You can dice or whisk the batter with the best of them.

At one point ... pass out .....

Give the guests numbers!

Samples!

<u>Evens</u>: Serve ... Prepare coffee ... drinks

<u>Odds</u>: Pick up ... Replenish ... Offer dessert.

All clean at the end. It may not be clear what to do at several points during the party. There may be fake or real mix-ups ... They may forget who has what assignment ... or they may not care. *I do it my way.*

A bit of confusion is colorful! Too much tradition is tiresome.

Let them ... sit anywhere, except in the bathroom! On the counter ... floor ... corner ... sturdy table ... even a chair. I prefer "his" lap.

Just give and take heed that they are <u>at</u> <u>home</u> and <u>happy</u>!

Like potato salad ... Share it ... and you have a picnic.

—Sam N. Hampton

You might omit having them scrub pans or take out the rubbish bag ... unless they offer.

But *tout le monde* desires to take home a doggie bag!

A mooch for a smooch! Ouch! Yes, that was a big flaky ... but <u>fun</u>!

And that's what it is. You may fancy this is a sparkling finale ... but it's really ready-made for an encore that never ends.

How candied to chase ... egg on ... honey up ... nip ... stuff and tie on the feed bag. All will join in the joviality ...

especially the joker. Flit about ... overflowing with friendly ferment.

Good <u>night</u>!! <u>No</u> .... good-byes! <u>Now</u> .... hale and hearty <u>hellos</u> and <u>hugs</u> ... Move and melodize to the mood of the music.

You'll be rewarded with recognition ... because you awarded them with merriment and memories ... and a doggie bag.

Your soirée was more spruced up ... than a set ... standard ... stockroom. You socked it to them with hospitality and hullabaloo ... instead of ho-hum.

But you're not a gourmet yet! You're still at the booming baby blue ribbon stage. You now have to go for the bronze ... silver ... and gold ... the whole enchilada ...

I admit I did a bit of apple polishing to butter you up ... but you still are a green vegetable.

If a is a success in life, then a equals x plus y plus z. Work is x, y is play, and z is keeping your mouth shut.

—Albert Einstein

And <u>especially</u> that last recipe when it comes to passion fruit.

And it does take <u>work</u> ... to play. In your salad days ... you were thin ... watered-down ... and dry behind the ears.

But <u>now</u> ... you're ready to drop a dash (and more later) of succulent creamy dressings ... all flavors. Break that tradition and crow!

You won't become a fat hen or a raging bull ... but rather the toast of the town to yourself and others ... because you know how to cook up a storm without burning the toast. There is no such thing as a bad performance if you give all but the kitchen sink ...

What the blazes am I puffing about? Stick to your capers before the tarts!

Er ..... don't eat a donut that has holes!

Do you get the message? No? Namely ..... Don't make a mess ..... and you won't have to clean up. Try to sort out and select the right recipe and ingredients. Be ready!

A clear broth is easier to digest than falling in a stew and beefing about it.

Before you raise cane ... catch on to what character you are ... and why you're producing this particular party. Whatever the reason ... coat well with sugar and spices. Never with chili sauce.

Timing

A widespread formula is to have appetizers from 6 to 8 p.m. Why stand for that? Don't set your room temperature like everybody else. Cool it ... or heat it up ... at 6 to 8 a.m. ... 11 p.m. to 2 a.m. ... 2 to 5 a.m.

As Marlene Dietrich coooood ... *If you're not free in the evening ... the afternoon will do!*

And serve immediately. Why keep that mystery item a secret? Show him/her ... what you're made of. Are you—they ... hot off the griddle ... simmering ... or chilled? Start preparing and sifting the flour.

Your party of two or more is to charm ... capture ... conquer ... like you never dreamed you could.

Stop being marshmallow fluff or mashed potatoes. Be chewy caramelized popcorn ... and sizzling steaks.

This is the Jet Age ... No more circling around ... zoom forward ... and <u>square</u> off ... for a smooth landing without a spill.

I'm not referring to TV dinners or takeout pizzas. Too easy! Too pasty and bland. No challenge or creativity. A snap of the fingers ... it's gulped down quickly—and tastes awful cold.

Cue time ... Quality ... Quantity ... Quest ...

To me, the choicest cut and the way to be in the thick of things ... is <u>home</u>-style chuck. Chuck ... that sticks to your ribs.

Mankind is divisible into two great classes: hosts and guests.
                                            —Max Beerbolm

The hostess with the mostess, or the host who can create the most.

Women! Invite only men. I did! I whipped up a tidbit that several men were in love with me. Several dipped into my ditty and farcical fancy ... for several rehearsals. They gobbled my tasty relish and weren't skittish about my skit.

Everything was above the counter ... and the men were <u>all</u> prime cut and prize bulls. Eventually ... I invited <u>some</u> women to put their finger in the pie. But since I created this platter ... the bulls gave me the prize ... and it wasn't dirty rice.

Several times I'm also invited to play bridge with three (3) men.

There is nothing fishy in anything I do. You should take any bait you can tackle ... Just know when to get hooked in.

Dates ... again ... dry. He's succulent ... smooth. She's honeyed ... polished. Both are creamy cheese and very sweet to each other. Either way ... very sticky!

Be careful of what the seeds inside those dates can lead to ... It's much yummier when they are combined with another ingredient ... especially <u>homemade</u> bread.

Remember, at home, you rule the roost, and there are no rules except decency and decorum; otherwise, the meal is ruined. Coat well your ideas ... ideals ... and imagination. Eventually, you'll make your own bread.

If you want to turn out a delectable dish ... you must be one too! And a tray of tempting hors d'oeuvres may appear appetizing but may be difficult to eat ... sloppy and not satisfying. You wonder why you started it ... and how to digest it.

But not with:

Lorraine's ..... All-Original ..... Licks and Lures.

Let's crop up with a carousel for two. This is not at the crush or trying to catch stage ... but rather ... converse your preserve.

Raw Oysters

Raw oysters are supposed to stimulate ... They're a substitute. Sure, all these extras I've given you ... seem so too ... they enrich and raise ... but oysters stand ... for what they are ... raw!

Keep them out of your spreads. Instead ... take them out of their shells and cream them with pearl onions.

Thoroughly drain the onions ... and drop them ... one ... by ... one ... into a saucepan of one cup of cream and one cup of half and half. Cinnamon or nutmeg, if desired. Yes ... it is very rich and thick.

Lightly sauté six oysters ... Then smooth them in the pan ... with the onions ... verrrrrrry slowly ..... Both stir and stir together. Don't let anything ... burn. Be wise to place wire underneath pan.

When you think you're ... er ... it's done ... at a snail's pace ... holding a ladle high ... drip into one deep plate.

Before: Heat several pieces of garlic (or plain) buttered toasted French bread slices.

With each slice, you or your guest ... swirl it around and around ... starting at the top ... like a whirlpool ... go lowwwwwer—and lowwwwwer — until you snag an oyster on the bread … Take it out and have him/her nibble at it. It can be finger lickin' good. Repeat … but reverse roles.

Anyone will turn green with envy or spoony when you butter them up … make them sizzle … sauté … and serve …

Six Steaming Oysters … with Ruby Red Sauce.

Soooooo colorful!

Saucy sauce:

1 can of plain or garlic tomato sauce
1 egg
1 tablespoon sugar
1 teaspoon piquant sauce
½ onion, finely chopped

Mix together ingredients and heat thoroughly.

Cagily, put the heated steamed oysters in their beds … their beds … and pour sauce in bowl.

Let your one lie on the floor (only) with pillows underneath the head … and place the tray of oysters and sauce … beside the pillows. You kneel beside tray.

Fork an oyster and slowly and seductively … thoroughly dip oysters into red mixture; quickly put it in his/her mouth. It may drip on their nose ….. so what! Kiss it off. Repeat and repeat ….. Then change positions. Any way you want.

A sip of white wine now and then would be ideal.

Kayma with a Kick
(Steak Tartar)

Now .... this appetizer is very raw!

This is delicious for having a tête-à-tête ...or at a sizable soirée.

Pitch in finding:

Large bowl	Small serving bowl
Large platter	Small serving ladle
Ice cream scoop	Large, flat flatware
Medium-size saucepan	Small mixing spoon
Dicing knife	

Plus:

One pound of top of the round
and lean leg of lamb (trim the fat) ... ground twice
½ pound small cracked wheat (bulgur)
Chili sauce
Onion juice
Dried parsley
Garlic powder
Small pitcher cold water
Piquant sauce
Salt & pepper

Two onions
Fresh parsley
Radishes
Cold cooked Brussels sprouts
Party-sized rye bread

Mayonnaise
Sweet pepper relish
1 can clear chicken broth

<u>Prepare the first set of ingredients up to the drawn line …
for kayma.</u>

Have some take turns at kneading.

<u>Knead</u>, I say … clean hands … warm heart … or wear light
plastic gloves.

Place large bowl containing all the meat in the sink or on a
round table. Two people stand with their hands in bowl.

Several others form a semicircle around them. Each one
holds the ingredients mentioned and pours them into the
bowl — to taste … and as kneaded.

The couple vigorously squashes the mixture. There could be
switching of roles — so everyone has their hand in it — but
remember … better wear gloves.

There could be kissy … kissy … a jig … a dance … each
adding their own touch and makings to the tune.

Or singing of the Anvil Chorus.

Tuck-tuck here … stuff-stuff there in the "Merry Old Land
of Oz."

Old MacDonald had a farm …. E-I-E-I-Ooooooooooo! With an
oink … oink … here … and an oink … oink … there … here
an oink … there an oink … everywhere an oink! oink! etc.

Or another course ... The host has Armenian décor ... props ... and music ... and all ... oscillate!

Others can dice onions ... decorate radishes ... prepare sprouts ... parsley ... bread.

In a small bowl ... two can make it ... with mayonnaise ... sweet relish and chili sauce ... to form Russian dressing. Then pour it on ... in a fancy dish.

When the meat mixture is good enough to eat and firm ... scoop with an ice cream scoop and pyramid onto a platter. Decorate with chopped onions on top ... Circle the platter with parsley ... sprouts ... radishes and bread. The Russian dressing is on the side ... if they want to spread on bread before putting on kayma.

Serves 15-20.

If any is left over ... rare ... or raw ... ha ha! ... cook with chicken broth ... until they rise to the top. Hot or cold ... you're right on ...

Cabbage Patch Cajolery

This could be extremely offensive ... or foul ... (but ohhhh so good) ... if ... you don't boil the cabbage ... until tender ... the day before. Also ... have a puff of air in the room.

Don't forget a drop of oil in the water ... and when done ... drain and refrigerate.

The next day ... stand it at room temperature.

Separate the leaves ... Peeling ... could be done with two or more ... It's your choice.

Take the paper towels and put a leaf in between ... you pat one towel with the palm of your hand ... your sweet or dear ... on the other ... and rub! Repeat ... or let others do it ... until it ... you ... and they ... are perfectly dry. If this step takes a stretched-out time ... who cares? Making the meal ... is just as enjoyable as eating it. Waiting whets ... while licking the lamb chops. The trend today is to be cool ... well ... cool it!

And add these stuffings when ready.

<u>Caviar</u> <u>Cabbage</u> <u>Cupcakes</u>

Carefully cut each cabbage leaf into halves. Spoon caviar onto each slice and place in <u>tiny</u> cupcake wrappers.

Pull one corner of wrapper down and either you seductively lick and eat the "cupcakes" ... or you feed it to <u>the</u> one ... to nibble on. If you, yourself, are a cupcake ... don't give it a go.

<u>Or</u> ham it up!

Slices of cooked ham ... How much? ... What kind? I can't tell you <u>everything</u>! Grind in blender with ...

Hot pepper relish
Mayonnaise
Onions ... pickle juice ... if you dare

Each one of you ... plop this mishmash onto a cabbage leaf ... and roll up firmly. Let it ooze out as you feed each other.

Do the same with other concoctions:

1. Cooked yellow rice with raisins
2. Brie or cheddar cheese melted
3. Meatballs
4. Sautéed mushrooms and onions
5. Cooked tomatoes and olives
6. Deviled egg mixture

Note: What to do with the other part ... the white of the egg ... of course ... I'll egg you on later! Ouch! Oh well!

7. You might get gooseflesh when you mash strawberries and blueberries with fingers ... Blend with whipped cream cheese ... I hope you use a bowl and spoon ... Then dollop on cabbage ... Roll up ... and gobble it down ... nibble delicately or make a gooey mess.

Foxy Fondues

All singles should buy a fondue set! Why? Because there are so many fair ways you can fondle with fondue flavorings.

Only for ongoing relationships.

Just fancy the two of you ... on the floor ... opposite each other ... with the fondue set in between. The only light is from the crackling fireplace. What mysterious and magic spells you can conjure up with the concoction.

You could be a fortune teller, and the fondue set could be your crystal ball. You are both slowwwwwly stirrrrring ... with fantastic fantasies.

Bubble, bubble, toil and trouble.

The only trouble you'll find is if you forget to light the burner underneath.

For you <u>others</u> who don't have a sweet potato or yam ... you can still fashion yourself ... as a fortune teller and feed each other ... but everything is on the table and aboveboard.

You can pour on the sauce with these!

Countless types of cheese ... with or without wine.
Chocolate
Cream ... plain ... vegetables ... or fruit.
Jelly ... jam ...
More

With:
Cooked shrimp or lobster
Cooked eggplant or turnips
Pearl onions
Cherry tomatoes
Marshmallows
All fresh fruit
Cooked crepes—<u>not</u> toasted ... so much softer to the taste.
More

Crepes are another chip almost in the same block.

Pigs in a blanket ... hot dog.

Pig in clover ... fruitful fulfillings

Pig in a poke ... Risk the unknown.

Like fondue, the recipes and how to make it ... are too numerous ... as stars in the Milky Way ... but since you are becoming a star ... I won't baby you.

(The baby) romped on my lap like a short, stout salmon.
                    —Sylvia Townsend Warner

You know what to do with fish that's left over too long!

And speaking about leftovers! Nooooo! Not your old flame ... those eggs!

Jam pack them with caviar ... cooked sausage ... bacon ... cheese ... crabmeat ... or the kitchen sink.

Scrambled with:

A yogurt dressing.

Plain yogurt ... chopped raisins and dates ... a dab of mayonnaise.

Lorraine's All-Original Lazy Licks

They're a snap ... snappy ... and snapped up.

1. Roll tuna fish salad around seedless red grapes ... Have toothpicks handy ... or the hell with them.

2. Peanut butter ... finely chopped onions, mayonnaise ... on crackers ... It's delicious.

3. Saltines with a chunk of pineapple and cherries on top. Maraschino cherries only.

4. Thick banana slices with sweet or hot pepper relish on top. Talk about whetting the appetite ... You should also have wet cloths.

5. Cold bought bean dip or paté spread on a long, thin graham cracker. If it's too dry ... halve it ... and dip it in yogurt or champagne.

6. Two sardines inside a celery stalk with a thin layer of honey mustard. If you want to be fresh ... hold your head back and savor the sardines to drop in your mouth. Or lick them.

7. Cut gherkins in center ... and stuff them with chive cream cheese. To make it sweet and sour ... add a slice of dill pickle. That ought to cuke you.

8. Chicken salad mixed with (sweetened or all-natural) raspberry jam ... served on a toasted bite-sized bread ... no crust ... sweat ... tears.

   Sometimes it's sophisticated to be simple—<u>sometimes</u>!

9. Everyone savors Armenian string cheese. Always soak it in water first. Naturally, I mean the cheese ... Oh well ... do what you want!

   And have fun pulling ... <u>the cheese</u> ... apart into very fine strings.

   You might smack your lips more ... if you take one end ... and your select ... takes the other ... and finally ... you know ...

10. Put into practice <u>your</u> pretty kettle of fish.

Time now to change one's tune and bang at that kettledrum and clash those cymbals to be .....

An exotic entrée.

Man-Slaying Hector's Farewell to Eggplant-Cooking Andromeda

Chapter IV

EXOTIC ENTRÉES

Are you ripe enough for this? Or are you still a fast-order cook ... who only knows how to steam up a fish story ... and be mushy or tart?

To be a gourmet chef, you must have the right ... tried and true recipes ... that you choose and handle with care. They are the most flavorful. Many times it tastes better the next day ... even if it's turkey ... and terrific when mixed ... diced ... ground ... stirred ... folded ... blended ... with spices.

Take pride with your prized toppings ... so that you can lay it on thick and not be so thin and starchy. Grin and give ... rather than bare it all the time.

If you're such a smart cookie ... your hand wouldn't be in the cookie jar, but putting them on the counter to cool. In other words ... don't belly hop to the dessert.

You can make your exotic entrée into being an epicurean chef d'oeuvre. Fancy airs ... yes ... especially when the aroma is "good." And there's nothing wrong when you sprinkle powdered sugar and seasonings in your own soup.

Be cuisine instead of chow!

Beating again ...

Love <u>is</u> a business. And it's your business to do something about it ... especially where and how to market your product.

Didn't you cram and crew over the computer until you were crisp and that cookie yours?

Are you successful in your professional and social life ... or are you self-serving ... have the backbone of a banana or lack fizz ... and so you are fizzled out?

Wellll?? If you want to change your ingredients ... have a fun feast.

For a sample dinner ... let's blend the two!

You want to make a splash for your special squeeze ... boss ... or client.

The run of the mill groove is not groovy.

They enter ... You greet them ... serve drinks and "nice" hors d'oeuvres in the living room ... dine "nicely" with "nice" conversation ... manners ... attire ... and the evening is "nice" and normal.

I'm <u>sure</u> they will remember that evening for the rest of their lives. Oh, yesss!!!

You might as well have opened a can of beans. Not even a can of worms for bait. You hooked them with a guppy ... instead of a whale of a time ... good enough to eat.

Bowl them over ... <u>immediately</u>!!

1. A bubbly chestnut or topic of today.
2. Create a cracker barrel or cracker jack original.
3. A poppycockish present.
4. If he/she relishes a celebrity ... curry the flavor
   for them.

Sure, this is pouring on the ketchup ... So what? ... It's for
them. But don't spend like water ... more like chicken feed.

Above all ... don't be scraping or smooth-tongued ... but
pure stock.

Another sprinkle:

If they are from a foreign country, or you're savvy that they
savor their heritage ... they'll be pleased as punch ... if
you ...

1. Lumped together one or two foreign expressions.
2. Tiny dolls ... flags ... banners ... posters or
   music.
3. A taste of Americana. Tell them what's in the
   chips now.

Show them you're more than a spoonful ... by dipping into
spoonerisms ... and whisk them into the kitchen.

Only be spoony ... with your snookins.

If your kitchen is small potatoes ... put them at the
entrance. Why should you dash back and forth? Let them
rub elbows with you ... but not elbow grease ... or rub them
the wrong way. It should be a bull session ... not shooting
the bull.

And don't dish the dirt … scrub the pan dry … or do your scraping and polishing in front of them.

Spill over with moxie. If you do … they will melt with your mood.

If your kitchen's good sized … create a charming setting with rare décor … candles (in a safe area) … small tables … a high chair. They mostly will be standing … lighting the candles … opening the wine … and quickly munching on your hot, heavenly hors d'oeuvres bubbling from the microwave.

How about telling each other's fortunes … every time they swirl a delicacy around the fondue set … (or maybe at dessert time).

Scramble for them <u>now</u>! If you show your sharpness on the <u>spot</u> … it sets the stage … so your soirée can never be dull.

The menu is now for them to take the candles … wine … salad into the dining or living room.

Another jarring!

Who says you must serve salad? It can be before the meal … during … after … or not at all. You could have a colorful variety on a platter, with two kinds of dressings … regular and fat-free on the side … or in the center of the table. Just pour it on.

Then … you wouldn't have to pop up and down like a sponge cake.

While in the kitchen … you can uncover to your guests your culinary house special … by letting them blend and mix.

You'll <u>always</u> have the right recipe ... because you <u>made</u> your house a <u>home</u>!

And roll it over ... to the outside. Too bad some charities ... politics ... churches ... organizations ... schools ... are overstuffed with clusters of cliques. Show them you won't be sandwiched in, and you're going to grow by harvesting a <u>mint</u> crop and being a fun raiser for their fund raising. You'll never be a garden variety again ... but an exotic entrée.

Oh ... yes ... your dinner. Let the timer bell remind you ... It's not <u>what</u> you serve ... but <u>how</u> you serve "it" up! Ham it up ... as long as you don't act like a goose.

Eat up the road with these table talk quotes.

A little sincerity is a dangerous thing, and a great deal of it is absolutely fatal.
—Oscar Wilde

If you are ever at a loss to support a flagging conversation, introduce the subject of eating.
—Leigh Hunt

At a dinner party one should eat wisely but not too well, and talk well but not too wisely.
—W. Somerset Maugham

The opposite of talking isn't listening. The opposite of talking is waiting.
—Fran Lebowitz

And pleasssseeee—don't admit you are so stale as to put fresh flowers in the center of the table! <u>That</u> ought to lick their chops ... I thought your salad days were over.

If you think squash is a competitive activity, try flower arrangement.

—Alan Bennett

Easy as pie ... Toss or drop them ... on the floor (not to trip) ... table ... picture frames ... mirrors ... lights ... or design and display them on the walls.

With your sweetheart only ... one or more in your hand ... or teeth. That'll go like hot cakes and raise their yeast. Olé.

So would red ... yellow ... and blue lights only! Oleo—oleo—entry.

You might spin things around with a lazy Susan ... in the center or side table, with a colorful array of fruits and vegetables ... encircled with seasonings or dips.

A fruit is a vegetable with looks and money. Plus, if you let fruit rot, it turns into wine, something brussels sprouts never do.

—P.J. O'Rourke

Or at dessert time ... have your guests make their own sundaes. You scoop the ice cream ... and they swoop on raisins ... nuts ... bananas ... sauces. Optional ... whipped cream and cherries.

More scoops on desserts later ... but you can never go flat with fresh fruit.

My original fancy ... I'm full of them ... so you will be ...

Have an arrow (cardboard or paper) protruding out at the edge of the lazy Susan. Each one takes turns twirling it ...

and guessing where the arrow stops ... person ... wall ... window ... door ... chair ... etc.

Best guesser wins a booby prize. But if your company is cold ... and a clam chowder ... don't take a crack at it. You rule ... I'm cocksure Judge Judy would be game.

Why don't you toss out juicy tidbits that are comical or from connoisseurs on horoscopes ... especially your visitor's birthday. Who doesn't relish their own visions?

At my gala ... the cookie crumbled when I conjured up multi-colored fortune cookies. More curry was powdered ... when they punched out their <u>own</u> snappy concoctions and cute creations.

Or they might discover (again ... my own discovery) ... a decorative puffy package ... or several king-sized to small-sized ones ... on the dining or side table.

Don't let anyone peek underneath the box until you're ready. Talk about steaming or brewing a tempest in a teapot.

1. A murder mystery! Spoon-feed and sprinkle the script <u>lightly</u>! The clues are in each box ... and the murderer at the end. You may start with the large one — or reverse it.

2. Whoever makes you belly laugh with the best fish or fishy tale.

3. Twenty-one questions ... so you can uncover the peach-dandy prize.

4. Your <u>own</u> punch line.

It could be at dinner ... dessert ... or both. It's your cream of the crop.

You might put stock in ... that you'd be in a pickle ... if you don't steer to the topic of ... bread and butter.

Pull the Columbo ploy. I did ... and successfully ... when on the stewardship for my church.

They're sharp to the reason of this gathering ... soooooo ... garnish ... and go down the garden path ... on every branch ... but ... business!

When they're on their way out ... you say ...

Oh ... by the way ....

Then pitch like a hot potato ... as you whip up their doggie bag ... a recipe they might want ... the remaining or a new bottle of wine.

Be bubbly as champagne ... and make it sound natural ... or you'll be the leftovers.

The right recipe kneads to be rehearsed and rehearsed! Practice makes perfect!

Let's turn the tables back to your fine dining! It's exotic entrées ... if the flavor is prime and choice cut ... hits the spot ... and tastes just right.

Show off ... but with sprinkles ... splashes ... spices ...

And not dampen ... drown ... or douse with vinegar or store-bought dressings.

If you're homemade ... homespun ... and make them at home ... hurray!!!

You can also be "at home" in a restaurant ... career ... social ... shopping ... travel ... because you know how to cut the mustard. Others will pick up on your ... creative crop ... let them!

You are beginning to be a rare roast ... creamed corn ... goose-stepping to harrrrrvarrrrrd—beets ... and a loving cup.

Dash and dip more about how to sweet talk to them so they will be your honey bun.

They could be saccharine ... sugary ... caramel ... custard ... taffy ... glucose ... peanut brittle ... nougat ... a lollipop or a mint ... you still love that bonbon.

How to make your potluck relationship into a bon vivant? Keep stirring ... or it will boil over ... or dilute.

Don't dash ... toss ... or swallow hard. <u>Plunge</u> in ... but then ... be

Creeping like a snail.
                              —Shakespeare

Tackle ... but then let them try to catch you.

And <u>why</u> ... should he or she pick <u>you</u> ... out of the crop? Are you a juicy plum or a rotten tomato?

Is <u>he or she</u> a hot tamale, a cold fish or a blue plate special?

If you're mushy ... you're nothing but mush in anyone's hands ... You can't spoil a can of mushroom soup ... unless you or the milk is sour.

You don't have to serve pheasant under glass ... you can mug it up with frankfurters to be a hotdog.

It's better to be looked over than overlooked.

—Mae West

Yes!!!

Are you washing this down? ... or haven't you taken a sip? Are you overflowing and overfilling your cup ... or is it water off a duck's back! That cereal doesn't snap ... crackle ... pop ... until you pour on the cream!

Be naughty but nice ... not nasty and nippy.

A man in the house is worth two in the street.

—Mae West

Annnnd ... at home!

Skip rope ... My mother told me to add the onions ... garlic ... mustard ... ginger ... ketchup ... nutmeg ... cloves ... sage ... thyme ... salt and pepppppperrrrr!!!

If you're peppery ... you can't be a dilly ... who dillydallies. You can wax into a tasty dish ... snap to it ... and you won't be a turtle.

From a meatloaf to a roast that's in the pink ... basting over and over — but no beefing or lambing.

Then your churning will melt in anyone's mouth.

Your dinner cannot be spoiled if you shine and are polished … and a bit dippy … Yes … dippy <u>do</u> … can be a delight … even if your dinner is a disaster.

Your steaks come out tough … you burn the crepes … or you can't even scramble an egg.

So what?? Ham it up!!

Prepare store-bought cold cuts and sandwich your amorist between a sweet pickle and a smile. Or even … swing to a square dance. You <u>can't</u> lay an egg … because …

Let's all crow together …

It's not <u>what</u> you serve … but <u>how</u> you serve "it" up!!

Your crepes burn … (not more than one … if <u>done</u> on purpose) … Don't clam up … or crab … Be sexy … smooth … and <u>sing</u> … as you scrape off the crust or "make" one together.

<u>Together</u> … There's the rub … and if you pull a boner … or boo-boo … go on … boo-hoo … Even <u>doughy</u> men do … Yes … they do. And I don't mean moneyed men.

Let <u>your</u> one … rub … lick … or spoon with you. Your yoke will be more fused and flow more easily unless he or she is a frozen flounder or a chowder head. Then … why bother.

If they're late …

I have noticed that the people who are late are often so much jollier than the people who have to wait for them.

—E.V. Lucas

You know what charm is: a way of getting the answer yes without having asked any clear question.

—Albert Camus

Don't be bitter ... Whisk them into the kitchen ... and set them on a high chair ... Put a bib ... towel ... napkin ... or aluminum foil about their neck ... and rub noses ... massage ... or wolf them down with goodies.

While you're frittering away ... play the Johnny game. One of my favorites.

Hold up your left hand ... and with your right forefinger .. tap your pinkie ... and quickly go to the others and say ... Johnny ... as you touch each finger. Before your thumb ... swoop ... and say ... whooooops ... and then touch your thumb ... saying ... Johnny.

Go back with <u>no</u> swoops ... whoops ... and touch the other fingers ... always saying ... Johnny. Then ... <u>very</u> ... <u>very</u> ... subtly ... fold your hands in your lap.

It's best to do ... when you are sitting. You can can-can about while <u>they</u> play.

Those repeating ... always put an extra Johnny at the thumb ... or an extra swoop.

Rarely, <u>very</u> rarely ... do they catch you folding your hands on your lap at the end.

It's fun for them to figure you out … in more ways than one.

Gals:

Don't ask me why … but most men love gin rummy … maybe because it's quick and easy … Ouch! Yes … I tossed that out. You … too!

Before … during or after your munchies … play your cards right into his hands … and play to win … Men love a challenge!

Or play your own hand or tune … but play!!

Men:

Some women don't want you in the kitchen … You're in the way! Pleasssse … don't tell me who they are.

Show her you can be a turn-on at stirring or peeling … especially a grape.

At each round … when your snookins finishes … pinch hits … dicing … or setting things up …

Kitchy … kitchy … koo … in the kitchen … but not in the sink or stew.

Lorraine's Original Latest Levity

So you're hung up that you're a chicken or a turkey. You've hung up your chef's cap and rung down the curtain …

Don't produce to me … You can't. You'll only be canny. Be a jar! Sow the seeds … it takes time to plant and grow! Don't go at a snail's pace. Sure ... you'll find plenty of worms in the ground ... Dig them out ... and dig in.

Seek and ye shall find.

—The Bible

But you won't ... if you don't use the right fork ... and have the party spirit.

Two synonyms for give ... are *backer* ... and *angel* ...

Now get <u>real</u> ... with that chicken or turkey.

Be Cool Not Callow with Chicken

He's there ... and she's there.
And both seem to care
To be savoir-faire.
And they glare and stare
At a chicken who's bare.

Don't be sheepish ... as you both smother the chicken or turkey with butter ... or seasonings. But don't spread too much on ... A light touch will do. <u>Always</u> put a lid on ... when baking the bird. Believe me, it comes out tender.

Half-baked ... (at 350° ... and one hour later) ... Yes ... This time ... open the oven and take off the cover. It may be steaming a bit ... so be careful.

Drain the juices ... fat ... and add ... any vegetables you want ... potato ... squash ... onions ... carrots ... peppers ...

One-half hour later ... check again ... and smooth on ... cranberry relish ... or ... grape jelly.

Wait a few minutes ... before you do ... otherwise ... you'll get a boo-boo! And boo-hoo! Oh ... Do it anyway.

Of course, a turkey takes longer to cook up a storm and a tie that binds ... so be patient. To microwave is much shorter... but it's really for the birds.

With you <u>both</u> holding a spatula ... prepare on a large platter and serve.

<u>Slice</u> it?? Forget it!!! Thin ... perfect pieces are tooooo perfect.

Give me a <u>chunk</u> any day ... tastes better ... <u>much</u> better!

There's nothing more delicious ... than devouring or dipping into sauce ... and being saucy. It's not fowl ... but finger lickin'.

Bingo!!! with Bulgur

You're worth a grain of salt if you say ... it is better to be <u>peared</u> than be <u>plum</u> alone.

Sauté red and/or green peppers. If desired ... four sliced onions—and/or mushrooms—a touch of garlic if you're on solid ground.

When almost golden brown ... break a handful of vermicelli into several pieces and put it into a medium-size saucepan with a small amount of oil ... and one cup of bulgur (cracked wheat) … Sauté until that is golden brown … on <u>low</u> heat … stirring constantly.

In the meantime … vigorously boil three cups of clear chicken broth … and when vermicelli is golden … add broth. Cook for one hour <u>without</u> mixing … on warm heat.

When done … add and blend pepper and onion mixture.

A very tempting dish … with chicken — turkey — steak or just salad.

Yellow raisins or cooked lamb chunks may be added as a feature.

<u>Go with Energy by Eating Eggplant</u>

After you both pat the eggplant's bottom … strip …

The outside layer … and cover with a towel … until completely dry.

You <u>know</u> … I mean the eggplant!

Slice in circles … then place some in a small roasting pan … cover with red tomato sauce. Then in alternating layers … add onions … peppers … carrots (or what <u>you</u> want) … and pour the sauce on every thing. But not <u>too</u> much.

You could top it off with slices of Swiss or cheddar cheese.

Bake at 350° with cover <u>on</u> … for one hour … or until bubbly.

This is <u>one</u> time ... it's getting <u>baked</u> <u>slowly</u> ... instead of <u>fried</u> <u>quickly</u>.

Note: I <u>never</u> ... <u>never</u> for <u>any</u> food ... <u>preheat</u> <u>oven</u>. Let the food and oven get to know each other.

Be Sappy with My Succulent Stuffing

Oh ... yes ... Here we go again ...

Sauté chopped onions ... peppers ... celery.

You could add chopped chicken ... turkey <u>or</u> beef livers. A small amount of livers and ... the poultry seasoning is better.

Heat one quart of milk (skim if preferred) ... in a large bowl—Crumble a long loaf of <u>fresh</u> ... <u>very</u> <u>fresh</u> ... white bread ... Add milk ... one raw egg ...

Mischievously ... be mushy ... with the mixture ... <u>and</u> with your main ingredient ... stir ... stir ... stir ...

At this time it's all right to be mushy.

Add the sautéed mixture into this mishmash ... Swirl it around ... and swing it into a casserole.

If your hands are squashy ... clean hands ... who cares how ... before you put the concoction in the oven ... 350° until bubbly ... You should be too ... You've got quite a dish ... there ... here ... and yourself aren't any worse for wear.

Where do we go from here?

To bed ... to trap ...

Ladida Luxurious Lobster

With <u>one</u> lobster ... you don't want to compete with a thing that's dressed all in red.

Instead ... sprout your own red herring ... by being the top banana.

If lobster is too rich ... <u>mug</u> it up ... even with frankfurters. Stretch not only your budget ... but yourself.

But one cooked lobster isn't going to break you ... You both ... are to break ... crack ... dunk ... and be buttery toward each other ... smacking your lips. You can lock horns as to who picks out the last piece as you both suck on a tail.

You can also scramble as you munch and crunch on <u>one</u> corn on the cob. Chaos? Noooo! Congeniality.

And don't you squares dare stew or sniff ... that everything I round out is hash or jammy.

You always can be spic and span ... courtly ... upper crust ... formal. But to be an exquisite ... enchanting epicurean ... you must have a farrago of toppings with frosting added.

Fun ... will make you home free.

You can pound that steak to make it tender ... or smother that fish with breadcrumbs ... but if it's tough to begin with ... all you have is a flat cutting.

By the way ... <u>bake</u> steaks and lamb chops! Bellissimo!!

And if that halibut is spoiled ... all the crumbs do is upset the apple cart.

<u>Smack Your Lips on Sexy Salmon</u>

Spouting about fish ... you must sip and bite this dish.

Salmon—cooked plain or with any spices you wish ... and then ... serve ....

In a <u>shallow</u> soup dish ... pour wine (prefer deep red merlot) ... into it.

Place the steaming hot salmon into the dish <u>with</u> wine.

With a <u>soup</u> spoon—you'll devour it like there is no tomorrow—so do it today!!

<u>Lorraine's Lazy Licks</u>

<u>You Flip, I Flip,</u>
<u>We All Flip for French Toast</u>

Any five-year-old can prepare French toast ... but since this book isn't for kiddish gloves ... I suppose you'll want to know how to throw it together!

Ingredients

1½ cups of milk
4 eggs
Dash of cinnamon
¼ cup sugar
8 slices of bread
Any fresh kind.

If you're thinking about other fresh things, it is plain you are not breadth-wise.

You need a non-stick pan ... wooden spoon or fork ... fork or eggbeater ... and a medium-size bowl.

Whisk eggs ... not too hard ... Add milk and cinnamon ... Blend.

Soak each bread slice in mixture and put in skillet on low heat. Turn after a few minutes. Then serve with:

	On the Side
Maple syrup	Bacon
Butter/oleo	Sausage
Chocolate sauce	Ham
Ice cream	Potatoes
Powdered sugar	Vegetables
Plain whipped cream	Fruit
Cream-milk	Any which way
Cream cheese	

You mount your own goodies.

This Cheese Will Never Stand Alone

Who doesn't relish grilled cheese sandwiches?

You can prepare them in a pinch, and they are penny-pinching.

Especially mouth-watering ... when you sandwich in tomatoes ... onions ... pickles ... ham ... tomato sauce ... crabmeat ... salsa ... mushrooms ... jam ... chopped pecans ... or even a chocolate bar.

Spread out more cheese ... and/or salsa or sauce ... so it overflows outside the bread ... when heated. Slower than the seven-year itch ... nibble the melted cheese around the crust without cutting the bread. Very ... very ... inviting.

Simple Socko Spinach

This one will drain you! But what taste!

Don't try it ... if you don't follow my easy instructions to a tee. One neighbor didn't ... and blamed me that I purposely left out an item. It's the routine that counts.

Wash the spinach and dry it.

Put it in a saucepan on low heat.

In the meantime ... sauté ...

You're so uncanny! Yes ... yes ... yes ... onions and peppers.

Drain spinach of water in sink at least twice before adding a small can of tomato sauce.

<u>Drain</u> at least ... <u>6-8</u> <u>times</u> <u>more</u>.

Return to heat and put in another can of tomato sauce—

The contents—<u>not</u> the can!

Heat ... (You might add an egg at this point.)

<u>Drain</u> onions/peppers of any oil ... and blend with spinach.

It's absolutely super-duper!

<u>Don't Crab—and Beans to You, Too!</u>

Heat store-bought crab or codfish cakes in oven slowly or the microwave.

Open a can of red kidney beans and heat on stove.

When both are done ... place and pour on the beans with the thick sauce over the crabcakes.

Yummy!! You be ... too!

<u>Night Not Day</u>

You be <u>the</u> one who lays out ...

Breakfast for dinner.

This may not be original … but in this topsy-turvy time … far-out is in.

You want your <u>one</u> to remember … you … don't you?

It's not far-out to pitch in a fade.

Who says cereal … eggs … muffins … juice is breakfast fare?

Break the ice. Show others you're the right recipe.

Are you ready for

Decadent desserts?

"I think you're confusing your feelings for me with your feelings for vanilla Swiss almond chocolate fudge sundaes."

Chapter V

DECADENT DESSERTS

Flavors for ....

Steady customers only!

Sugar and spice and everything nice ...That's what little girls are made of.

Men are also:

Spicy and sweet
And good to eat

By now ... you should be a hot fudge sundae or an orange-brandy-flavored soufflé ... No more a frozen mud pie or sponge cake!

In your boudoir
You can go far

With a dish chasing the spoon ...

And being spoon-fed ...

With soft or hard delicacies.

Of course ... the point is ... pudding ... puff pastry or a strawberry or two!

These tips ... may not be as easy as pie.

We all know desserts should be delicious ... delightful ... divine ...

But if you drool over or devour too quickly ...

Does the spearmint lose its flavor on the bedpost overnight?

—Billy Rose and Marty Bloom

Are you chewing bubble gum ... or ...

Blowing your bubbles in the bath or basin?

With suds ... or sparkling champagne?

Bursting balloons filled with beer ... can be sloppy ... so do "it" ... in the shower.

We all can be fresh ... saucy ... syrupy ... with layers of sticky icing!

A cherub ... with a piece of ... Madonna ... Shirley Temple ... Spanky ... Mel Gibson ...

Your piece of pie should be practiced ... have the proper precise proportions ... plus slight stirring and pressing of the dough ... which will make the outcome tender ... not tough.

Be light and even ... when rolling ... Don't make the edge too thin ... You need to trim ... your crust ... after the pastry is filled.

Heat up!

... One or two small pies!

Mmmmm ... the arousing aroma of pumpkin!

Fling a veil ... scarf ... tie ... or even aluminum foil ... on your head ...

Put the pie on top ... like a chapeau ... Attach it with a ribbon ... string ... or hold it in one hand. Knead I say ... your hair never touches the food.

Or fasten two small pies ... to each wrist ...

I wouldn't even suggest any other place.

Frolic foolishly about to your favorite rumba or folk-rock music.

Corny ... nutty ... applesauce ... yes!!!

But unbeatable!

If the bouquet of pumpkin doesn't get to them ... your burlesque will.

Eventually ... nip at the pies.

I said ... the pies!

Then ... dance in the dessert!

Imagination is more important than knowledge.

—Albert Einstein

That's true on any topic!

Just don't raise too much cane ... glazing ... or powdered sugar on top.

How sweet it is.

—Jackie Gleason

Squeezing the melon ... stirring the sauce ... savoring the magic ... together ... hits the spot!

Once a dish is hot ... keep it that way!

Smear it on ... to be smooth.

What counts and what you should be measured by ... is spoonerisms and snappiness.

But to be in the buff ... all the time ... is not buffing ... but to buffet.

Birthday suits should be suited to the occasion.

It's more suitable to be someone special ... every day!

But how ... to make them ... discover you ... or if they ... are a dessert?

Ahhhhh ... there's the rub!

Give a man a free hand and he'll try to put it all over you.

—Mae West

Women, too!

What looks delectable is not necessarily good for you. Why smack someone who's like apples and oranges to you?

Is "it" pleasing to the palate ... or does "it" leave a bad taste in your mouth?

Everyone to his taste, as the woman said when she kissed his cow.
— Panta Gruel

A kiss ... here ... a kiss ... there ... a kiss everywhere ... anywhere!

Or cherries or popovers dipped in honey. Maybe ... strawberries as earrings? That's something to nibble on.

How the cookie crumbles is up to you! Potluck never brings you gold ... especially if you don't give a fig.

Be thou familiar, but by no means vulgar.

— Shakespeare

If you bite your tongue ... and blow kissy after kissy
You'll find you and others ... won't be so prim and prissy.

Suppose they are a hard sauce ... and won't swallow! Are you sure you ... aren't the picky eater?

Did you pick the flavorable plate from the dessert tray? If you did ...

With the proper toppings ... you can unfreeze that raspberry ... because you're that sherbet ... who's in the limelight!

Once you whip up and taste the right recipes by decorating ... swirling ... coloring ... and put that frosting into peaks ... you can have your cake ... and eat it too!

If others try to blow out your candles ... still glow and sparkle! You're a delectable dessert!

Sometimes ... you don't feel like cooking ... Chew on a carrot ... a tender tomato ... a mushy mushroom!

For that crème de la crème ... just whip up cream ... and let them lick your spoon ... especially ... with a raspberry lady finger.

Always devour <u>any</u> dessert with a spoon! Much sexier ... especially ... a dessert spoon!

Arabian nights ... with 1001 dessert spoon ... ing ... décor ... dolling up.

I wish I could shimmy like my sister Kate.
She shivers like the jelly on a plate.
                                    —Armand J. Piron

The rule is, jam tomorrow and jam yesterday—but never jam today.
                                    —Lewis Carroll

Why not? Sometimes it's good to put jam on your face!

It's all how you peel that banana ... flake that coconut ... or shell the pistachios.

This isn't pillow talk ... but so what!

In a glamorous restaurant ... 16 singles gathered for a gourmet dinner. We had a room just off the main dining room ...

Everyone was "politely" conversing when I entered. A few minutes later ... loud laughter. Who <u>do</u> you suppose sparked it? After a while ... I said jokingly ... 'I'm bored with you men! I bet if I go into the main dining room ... (it was buffet style) ... I could come back with a tall sexy man!'

All chirped ... *Sure!*

I was at the dessert table when a tall ... sexy ... younger man spoke <u>to</u> <u>me</u>. <u>Yes</u> ... <u>he</u> <u>did</u>!

Quickly ... I stated ... 'Would you do me a favor?'

Quickly he said ... *Why not?*

'Follow me!'

Which he did. I bounced into the room and introduced him ... pouring it on.

He played the game. As he left ... he told me ... *Anything you want.*

Two men stated they were impressed ... and one spoke of it later.

For the birds? That's how <u>you</u> wing it. But this is one canary that won't fly away in the men's minds.

To wow ... outside ... or in!

Flavors improve as they blend ... chilling ... contents ... cooking ... chef d'oeuvre!!

You can spark your spark ... when you're in the know ... then ... you'll know ... where ... when ... and howwwww!!!

You're prepared to plunge in!

And say so soothingly ...

With all thy faults, I love thee still.
> —Cowper

Er ... that isn't quite right.

I have been faithful to thee, Cynara in my fashion.

> —Ernest Dowson

Maybe Shakespeare.

"I was adored once too."

<u>That</u> ... won't do!

I went down on one knee and dictated a proposal which my secretary faxed straight away.

> —Stephen Fry and Hugh Laurie

Away ... yes ... not up ... up ... and away!

Action speaks louder than words.

Action speaks louder than words, but not nearly as often.

Words don't mean a thing. It's the action that counts.

Actions lie louder than words.
>   —Pym 1628, Debate on a
>   message from Charles I

"Lie" ... Is it the core or the seed?

People don't talk in Paris; they just look lovely ... and eat.

>   —Chips Channon

Some of the best laid plans of men ... are women.

>   —Dr. Mervin Lynch

Here are some <u>actual</u> <u>layouts</u> ... of men and women:

1. One gal wants to be clad in a bikini ... and her favorite ... decorates her like a Christmas tree ... with every trinket he could find ... including buttons ... bows ... and rum bonbons.

   And then ... just see how she lights up.

2. A man is in a whirlpool ... with his spark ... while they swirl and float in a whirlpool bath ... enjoying soothing songs ... sounds ... champagne ... cheese and crackers ... among other things!

   Possibly a ducky-wucky!

3. A friend finds this very sexy! His date takes a splashy sip of liquor ... Then ... both kiss ... and <u>he</u> gulps down the drink.

That's mixing your juice and stirring at the same time.

4. One good-time Charlie wants to grab his girl ... and go to a tropical island and ... and ... and ...

   Dates ... bananas ... coconuts ... aren't always pitted ... peeled ... or what they're cracked up to be.

5. Several ... both sexes ... desire ... dinner ... served up to them ...

   With or without ... wear ... and tear ... or the wait!

   Oh ... <u>well</u>!

   <u>Rare</u> ... not raw ... is always ... romantic.

If you find the pear or peach ... not tender ... don't pound.

Brush with buffoonnery!

Or a sitcom!

Without humor, you cannot run a sweetie shop, let alone a nation.
                                        —John Buchan

Be a comic Carmen.
Be a clownish Casanova.

Her fan won't open ... keeps flipping it. And cigarette smoke makes her sick.

His cane won't work ... and he can't stick it.

She stumbles ... when she shuffles her cards.

He wasn't up to snuff ... and can't sneeze.

She puts a rose in her mouth ... and a thorn pricks her.

He gets a bee in his bonnet and bounces about ... the William Tell Overture is great for this ... slow movement ... then ... hi-ho Silver!

Pop the corn ... with gobs of butter and salt to be gobbled up.

Then ....

The silence .... <u>after</u> the storm!!

<u>Lorraine's</u> <u>Luscious</u> <u>Loverlies</u>

Ingredients are mine ... which you will soon pinch ... poach ... and dash off ... and whyyyyy not?

About that cake ... This is the item you've been popping up for ... If you follow directions ... by now ... you should be sifting through the <u>flour</u> ... and they're aching for your <u>two lips</u>. Ouch!

Aunt Helen's Yum-Yum Cake

It's yummy ... yummier ... yummiest!

1 cup raisins
1 cup sugar
1½ cups water
½ teaspoon cinnamon
½ teaspoon salt
6 tablespoons cocoa

Cook for 4 minutes.

Let it be cold.

(In other words ... cool it ... in the refrigerator.)

Then add:
2 cups flour
1 teaspoon baking powder
1 teaspoon vanilla

Smooth together while smooching together ... then pour into a circular cake pan.

(Don't forget to grease it slightly.)

(The pan ... the pan ...)

Bake 40 minutes in a moderate oven.

Don't wait ... Lick ... the bowl ... Then do a conga ... as you both ... clean at the sink.

Wiggle while you work ...

(But no jumping on anything ...)

When done ... turn upside down and cool ...

The cake ... you harlequin ...

This fancy doesn't need frosting ... or fanfare!

<u>No</u> <u>thin</u> <u>slice</u> ... or politeness will do.

<u>Split</u> it into more <u>thick</u> pieces and polish it off ... feeding each other.

Someone's going to smack lips for more ... more ... more ... when they taste this.

X ... this!

The greatest degree of desserts are either <u>round</u> ... perfect circle and crowning glory,

Or <u>square</u>!!

<u>Take</u> <u>note</u>:

To <u>make</u> a dessert ... there is <u>always</u> more than one ingredient!

Does that produce a sprinkling to you ... ?

Stop glancing at the candy counter at all the goodies ... wishing ...

If you are full of surprises ... you wouldn't have to look in ... They'll look out for you!

This next recipe may be difficult to dig ... but give it a go ...
It may be all the better to bite on.

Cream Kadaif
by Lucy Mardirosian

Cream filling

3 cups heavy cream
2 cups milk
½ cup sugar
½ cup cornstarch
¾ lb. butter (3 sticks)
2 lbs. Kadaif dough

Heat cream and 1 cup milk over low flame and add sugar.

When you add sugar ... always keep on low flame.

Combine the rest of the milk and cornstarch, and mix until
the cornstarch is dissolved.

Don't omit to mix together ... so you can all melt ...

Add slowly to hot cream, stirring constantly until you have
a consistency of heavy pudding.

If you stir constantly, you'll never be a heavy.

Allow to cool.

You be, too ... at all times.

Separate and loosen Kadaif dough by rubbing gently.

Oh, boyyyyy!!!

Add melted butter and work through.

It takes work to butter up ... the right way.

Put half of Kadaif on bottom of pan.

The Kadaif ... the Kadaif ...

Spoon cream onto dough evenly, up to ½ inch away from the edges of the pan.

When you spoon ... a half an inch is right on the edge.

Cover with the remaining Kadaif.

Don't put a lid on it ... just cover.

Press gently.

Pleasssse dooooo!!!

Bake at 450° for 20-30 minutes.

Ooooooo ... What to do in the meantime? ... I just <u>can't</u> imagine.

Let stand for awhile and pour warm syrup over and cover.

I hope you're covered and don't become sticky.

Use a 12 x 16" pan.

Any substitutes?

<u>Syrup</u>

3 cups sugar
1 2/3 cups water
1 teaspoon lemon juice

Mix ingredients in saucepan.

At this point ... a bit of lemon is needed.

When it comes to a boil, allow it to continue boiling for only 2 minutes and then remove from heat.

If you think I'm going to gloss over that ... you're dippy.

Nothing like Mom ... Always on the square ... <u>the</u> best ... This is just like her.

<u>Mom's Brownies</u>

No comments <u>this</u> time.

Everything room temperature.

1½ cups sugar
1 1/3 sticks of margarine or butter
1/3 cup cocoa
<u>little</u> Armenian coffee (pulverized)

Bring to boil until sugar is melted.

Let cool ... Add ...

4 eggs — one at a time (mixing by hand)
2/3 cup flour

1 teaspoon baking powder
2 teaspoons vanilla
dash of salt

If desired ... add chopped walnuts or raisins ... or both ... on top.

In a flat, slightly greased baking pan, bake at 350° for about 30 minutes.

Cut while warm.

Here comes Mother's little helper ... with her curls.

Lorraine's Paramount Pie

Also called ...

Lorraine Is Lazy

I buy ready-made crust.

It's what's in-between the sheets that counts.

And my filling is the cat's pajamas.

Or anything else you put on.

Put an apple in your mouth ... and make them munch away with you ... until you reach the same core.

Before or after you chew on this ...

1/3 cup granulated light brown sugar
2 tablespoons flour
½ teaspoon cinnamon

¼ teaspoon nutmeg
1 tablespoon butter, cut up
12, more or less, <u>Macintosh</u> apples

Mix everything together, except the apples.

Peel …

…the apples … the apples … the apples!

And this time, don't take a bite out of them … Slice … instead.

And drop them into a large bowl of water so they won't become brown.

Nooooo! You are <u>not</u> going to dunk for them.

Drain completely. Toss the apples with all the ingredients …

Mix the mishmash into a shell — of course … with a 9" pie dish under it.

Put another crust on top … Trim … and poke top.

Not to burn crust … place foil around the rim of pie.

Do <u>not</u> preheat the oven — and bake until bubbly and brown …350°

You'll never be second fiddle … because they always ask for seconds!

The pie! The pie! The pie!

I know no ways to mince it in love, but directly to say, 'I love you.'
— Shakespeare

Annnnnnnd ... speaking of mince ...

Lorraine's Millennium Mincemeat Ice Cream Pie

1 large jar mincemeat
2 tablespoons rum
1 quart coffee ice cream

1 9" pie shell (baked)
½ pint whipped cream
green food coloring (optional)

Mix mincemeat, rum, and ice cream.

Put into pie shell.

Freeze.

When ready to serve ... top with whipped cream. If holiday time ... do use green food coloring ... and decorate with a red candle in center ... surrounded by holly.

Mince could mean to hold one's tongue.

If things don't pan out ... don't panic ... It isn't a panacea ... Quit pandering ... like a pancake or sift into a state of pandemonium ... Survey the panorama ... Your panoply shouldn't be hidden in the pantry ... if you can't go for pantomime with panache.

While the delight is baking ...

Your delight and you sit and stare ... and don't say a word.

The first one to even grind or snicker ... must bite ... the dust and pay a prearranged penalty.

You can shake a leg ... make faces ... twitch ... do finger exercises ... use props ... but no ... touchy-wutchie.

You'll be bowled over with body language.

Naturally ... if you want to take a break from each other ...

You could cut the grass ... wash windows ... replace worn-out cabinets ... sleep ...

And if you're snappish with each other, don't tread too hard or too long ... or your treat will fall or spill over ... and you will have to clean the oven ... though it won't be so tough if you scrub together.

Now that you've cleaned up ... sweep away this ...

Aunt Helen's Never-Fail Chocolate Cake

Melt 3 tablespoons of butter in a saucepan.

It doesn't take long to butter up ... if it's real.

Remove from heat and add 5 tablespoons cocoa ... Stir until smooth.

Now where did you read that before?

Put into a bowl and add:

1 cup sugar
½ cup milk
1 cup flour
2 teaspoons baking powder
2 eggs

Spin and rotate until well blended.

Exactly!

Pour into greased cake pan (8 x 8") and bake at 350° ... for about 40 minutes. While on the back burner ... you might whip up an icing.

Mine is messy and might win a booby prize and frosty stares.

All I can do is lick ... and sloppily frost a cake.

But ... what's in my favor is ... it's more flavorable ... and "it's" homemade ...

<u>A messy cake is sexy</u>!

How many perfect pastries have you seen? Hmmmmm??

You'd be jarred that a topsy-turvy dessert can be a diamond in the rough. A sticky mess can cling you together.

Of course ... if you want a priceless pearl ...

_____

Mom's Cherished Cheesecake

2 8 oz. packages cream cheese
3 eggs
1 cup sugar
1 pint sour cream or yogurt
1 teaspoon vanilla

If yogurt is used, add ½ teaspoon baking soda

Grease round springform pan lined with graham cracker crumbs.

Topping ... your choice

Let cream cheese stand ... at room temperature.

Mix until creamy.

Add eggs ... one at a time.

Add sugar ... a little at a time.

Still mixing.

Fold in sour cream and vanilla.

Pour into pan.

Bake at 375° for 30 minutes.

When cool ... spring open and add topping.

She always ended her letters "Cheerio" and her recipes with ...

Happy eating—Cheerio.

"I love you."

In three words ... my mother and/or Shakespeare summed up how to develop into a <u>Decadent</u> <u>Dessert</u>.

And a jig and a jug of

Wine ... women/men and song.

"We're in luck. It's _white_ wine!"

Chapter VI

WINE ... WOMEN/MEN AND SONG

I was so damned sorry for poor old Corky that I hadn't the heart to touch my breakfast. I told Jeeves to drink it himself.

—P.G. Wodehouse

Some weasel took the cork out of my lunch.

—W.C. Fields

The less I behave like Whistler's Mother the night before, the more I look like her the morning after.

—Tallulah Bankhead

Do you cheer whoopeeeeee ... or whoooooops?

You could be the toast of the town ... if you whooped it up with cheerio ... anytime ... anywhere ... instead of being toasted with cheers ... morning ... noon ... and night.

We drink one another's healths, and spoil our own.

—Jerome K. Jerome

Sure ... we dive into decadent desserts ... but not a belly flop ... or on the rocks. If you aren't fussy ... there could be a full twist on you.

If things go awry
You don't need scotch or rye.

Are you juggling with a jigger instead of <u>being</u> a juggler doing a jig?

We've all been in the backwater. Bounce back! You don't need a chaser ... Instead, become a good mixer ... by being cozy ... cordial ... companionable.

If you laugh ... you'll never be lonely.

Are you playing a pinball machine that always tilts ... when you should tilt in all directions ... if you're on the ball?

I'm not a tea totler ... but ...

"T" time can be terrific ... tempting ... tasty ... try it.

... Especially with all those other <u>goodies</u> you serve.

But don't be a tempest in a teapot.

Rather:

"I'm a little teapot
Short and stout
Here is my handle
Here is my spout.
When I get all steamed up
Then I shout,
Tip me over and pour me out.
I'm a very special pot, it's true.
Here, let me show you what <u>it</u> can do.
I can change my handle and my spout.
Tip me over and pour me out."

Sing for your supper ... instead of drinking down your dinner. Be a smash hit ... instead of smashed.

If you cutely or seductively sing and act out that song ... out of the blue ... you'll <u>always</u> be in the pink.

This is not a layout in lavender ... but exposing ... your negatives.

This should not be you.

I only know two tunes. One is "Yankee Doodle" and the other isn't.
—Ulysses S. Grant

Ditties can capture your prize package ... especially while performing.

"Pop Goes the Weasel"

"Rock-a-Bye Baby"

"London Bridge Is Falling Down"

"Who's Afraid of the Big Bad Wolf?"

"Daddy's Little Baby Loves Shortnen' Bread"

"Rock-a-Bye Parade"

Rock to your own parade ... but march ... march ... march.

Opera ... Broadway melodies ... country westerns ... folk ... oldies ... hot off the griddle ... or steaming favorites.

If you can't sing ... be a humdinger with a hum ... Wet your whistle ... in other ways ... tweet ... tweet ... tweet.

The most sophisticated men adore "Baby take a bow" ... with my Marlene Dietrich or Shirley Temple voice.

You're packing up their troubles and yours in an old kit bag ... tossing them away ... singing ... smiling ... and sparkling.

A friend told me ... that professionals snickered at Arthur Fiedler ... when he popularized Pops. But people of all ages ... were more than pleased as punch to be part of the production ... and still do ... It's always a party.

Wave <u>your</u> wand to ring in a new year everyday ... to bring out the new you. But remember ... what rings like a chime may be a clang.

Extraordinary how potent cheap music is.
—Noel Coward

You can woo with a kazoo ... and pay the Pied Piper.

But wouldn't you rather conduct your own orchestra?

Swing an overture with a bit more jazz.

Otherwise:

Dumb as a drum with a hole in it, Sir.
—Charles Dickens

You won't be ... if you're a different drummer ... Just don't bang away without being in tune, or you'll crash your cymbals.

Go on failing. Go on. Only next time, try to fail better.

—Samuel Beckett

It's not what I do, but the way I do it. It's not what I say, but the way I say it.

—Mae West

As said ... if you can't sing ... swing ... If you can't swing ... shake ... If you can't ... sit there and sulk.

As Shakespeare's Puck would sneer ...

Oh, what fools these mortals be.

That Puck has pluck!

I go, I go ... look how I go ... Faster than an arrow from a Tartar's bow.

—Shakespeare

Be a straight arrow ... right on ... always on target.

Everyone has emotions and expressions ... No exceptions. We all can ... be tasty ... thirsty ... and a treat.

But most ... don't move!

Or think a drink in the hand is worth more than squeezing your sugarbush.

Don't put it on ice ... Clean out your cabinets ... or shelve it.

It won't be such a strain ... when you serenade ... because if you're full of steam ... you don't have to sweat it out ... wondering ... watching ... waiting ...

The best way to hold a man is in your arms.
—Mae West

He who hesitates is lost.
—Proverb

By and by is easily said.
—Shakespeare

What may be done at any time ... will be done at no time.
—Thomas Fuller

Sooooooo ... go ... goo ... goooo ... gooooo ... and you'll crop up as the nectar of the goods ... no matter what age!

I've been around so long, I knew Doris Day before she was a virgin.
—Groucho Marx

And, speaking of virgins ... the Ritz makes one of the best virgin strawberry daiquiris. But their latest ... with "juice" and juice is called cosmopolitan!

You still can be stylish if you order a soft drink. I do ... and no one calls me a softie ... criticizes ... or cares.

And it's still cool to sip cold beer or bottled water with your company ... at sports ... social events ... or at a café.

I'm only a beer tea teetotaler, not a champagne teetotaler.
—George Bernard Shaw

You can be in hamburger heaven with your crush ... orange, that is ... not lemon ... as long as you have moxie.

That's the tonic ... You need to <u>act</u> ... double-quick ... chic ... tick ... comic ... chivalric ... and jump over that candlestick.

You're the biggest fish in the pond ... because you know how to swim <u>up</u>stream ... and nothing can throw water on it.

Bring your animation anywhere ... yes ... even to a funeral get-together. They will be inspired ... and not miss their grief ... even for a few moments.

Naturally ... there are different degrees ... but if you're confident ... clear ... courteous ... bright-eyed and bushy-tailed ... (tail of a cat ... which fluffs up when an animal becomes excited) ... You could be lapped up.

One time, I was at a funeral of a close friend. The daughter and his brother had pain in their faces. I related an amusing story about us ... and noticed a gleam in their eyes. What a wonderful, warm feeling and bond ... we all had.

Sure ... kittens or tomcats love to scratch ... but they can also purr ... and adore being pampered ... Hmmmmm?

They also drink milk or cream ... but if they took a nip ... that puss would need heavy boots ... so it wouldn't tip over... It may tickle you to see the puddy tat tipsy and pussyfoot about ... but soon you'll feel sorry or stick in your paw ... er ... craw.

The weaker the drink ... the stronger the person.

Most are spirited by too much spirits ... instead of spirit. They believe this bestows to them all sorts of drive ... when instead it drives them into another direction ... dullsville and depression.

The shadow isn't the only one to cloud man/woman's mind.

Forget your false front and be a forerunner.

A drink does not drown care, but waters it and makes it grow faster.
—Benjamin Franklin

Cook up a storm ... not wild winds.

By now ... you should have presented yourself with an array of not only blue ribbons ... but all the colors of the rainbow.

Rollick around the rosy maypole instead of a merry-go-round.

You need a beach umbrella and a cool cucumber ... rather than a crunchy celery and a pee-wee parasol ... because you're the fancy thirst quencher. And friends will always want a refill.

There's no sand in your shoes ... or sun in your eyes ... no blistering or peeling ... because you put on a protective shield ... but still dare to dive in.

You're familiar with the waters ... and don't dog paddle or sit in one spot.

No matter where you are ... you, alone, should steer your own ship. There may be rough waters ... and you are tossed ... but soon it's smooth sailing.

No man is an island entire of itself; every man is a piece of the continent.
—John Donne

So wherever you cruise or plow the waves ... wear a Mae West ... (a life preserver jacket) ... Okay ... okay ... that punch was lukewarm.

But you can be a hot toddy.

You should spot land by now.

You'll become sicker ... quicker
Because brandy's not dandy
Wine is fine
When you dine
But do your mixing with spice
Rather than a nightcap with ice

The minister was visiting my mother and me. When I suggested serving wine ... my mother stated ...

—Is that proper?

—He can always refuse.

Not only did he relish the potable ... but we all rejoiced ... when we handed him the bottle to take with him.

That same minister ... started a group ... the Pairs and Spares. He served us an Italian dinner at our opening meeting ... and chianti.

He asked us not to tell our parents about the wine ... they might object.

I did ... though. Mom didn't mind and was so thrilled ... that I joined the group ... at her urging ... not mine.

—I'm never going to meet anyone at a church supper.

What a dodo! You wouldn't believe how many "wow" men I met at church (more on where to go ... later).

Note:

Must eat many a peck of salt together before the claims of friendship are fulfilled.

—Cicero

Sample the wine before you dribble and swallow down the entire decanter.

In other words ... lots of time. Instant doesn't taste half as good ... as made from scratch ... and fully prepared ... for togetherness.

Champagne or wine ...
Can be divine.

These are <u>the</u> only spirits I serve at my soirées, which are so spirited and bubbling ... they hardly touch the bubbly.

You should have heard the ooooohs ... when I put on the lamp with red bulbs ... giving the champagne glasses ... a colorful glow.

You can imagine if they became excited over my lighting ... what the rest of the evening was like.

<u>Not</u> <u>once</u> ... in all my festive occasions did anyone ... ever ... become high ... except on my entertainment.

Who declared that you must pour on the drinks? And that you <u>must</u> have a drink in your hand at all times?

Probably the same jester who ruled ... *Cereal for breakfast.*

You be a happy-go-lucky harlequin ... and fill your palate with a variety of paints.

Okay ... here I go again. You ... too!

It's not what you serve ... but how you serve "it" up.

They won't want to leave.

They won't ask for chicken if you prepare lamb.

Why not marinate your cuisine with wine ... rum ... vodka ... whiskey ... gin ... scotch ... It might enhance your exotic entrées ... That idea's more savory than your guests or you being stewed.

You'd be surprised ... a drop here and there ... is quite enough. It'll not only stretch yourself ... but your budget.

Cocktail parties ... is a <u>name</u>!

You may wear a cocktail dress to a wedding ... and black tie isn't the only material you bare ... er ... bear.

You don't serve ... they don't get.

Why not be mischievous Foo-foo the Maid ... or Talbot the Bashful Butler ... and garnish the role. I thought of Barefoot Baron ... but ...

Dress and buckle the way <u>you</u> want ... as long as you don't slip ... into too many belts! Instead ... belt it out.

You can't ... if you act like a musty old maid ... or a stuffy ... dry or wet lemon who needs a twist from sitting on his b——.

A party of one or two ... is really up to you.

A brain of feathers, and a heart of lead!

—Alexander Pope

All the things I really like to do are either illegal, immoral, or fattening.

—Alexander Wollcott

I left the room with silent dignity, but caught my foot in the mat.

—George Grossmith
Weedon Grossmith

Men: Your tulip is going to tiptoe in ...

Women: Your tip-top treads in ...

What do you do?

Noooo! Helloooos!

A kiss? Yessss ... but a bit overfed.

Sweep them ... with a broom ... Slap ... a mixing bowl at them ... and let them stir ... Grab their hips and conga ... and then whisk them into the kitchen or living room.

I realize you want your peachy relationship to be romantic ... refined ... reposed.

It won't happen ... unless ... you're happy ... heartfelt ... harmonious ... annnnnd ... histrionic.

When you're down to earth ... you should be up on what's real.

It's rewarding to realize ... that each place and person is remarkable ... Vive la différence!

Poetry and pretty words still work ... <u>but</u> ...

This is a world of visual ... variety ... and vitality.

To have one for the road ... you're not in the driver's seat.

That extra nightcap doesn't feel like a feather ... but a hard hat.

You must call the shots ... and chill it.

Every time you want to break open a new bottle, break into a song instead.

Corny ... yessss! But better than corn liqueur.

Pop your cork at yours or others' parties with creative concoctions.

You be the wink and twinkle that refreshes ... Yes ... that's a refill ... but not an old fashioned.

Freshen up yourselves ... Don't let anyone soak you up like a sponge!

We lived for days on nothing but food and water.
                                                    —W.C. Fields

You are the captain of your ship ... the lady or lord of your own castle ... who can charm ... capture and conquer.

A function where you meet people who drink so much you can't remember their names.

—Cosmo Sardo

By now ... they should crave and thirst for you ... because you're the filet mignon ... the frosting ... and more.

Paramount ... not portable. And, if they do think of you as any port in a storm ... you're not rowing in the same boat ... Better shore up, or you'll drift in the fog.

If you do nothing ... no one will notice.

Most men and women adore a sweetheart who's strong ... smooth ... sweet.

More desirable than any drink ... or bringing your own booze.

Both genders like to be led ... so lead!

Zoom ... zing ... zip ...

Tug at his tie ...

Massage her neck.

Both ... take in hand and ... grin like a Cheshire cat ... wink ... or once in a while, peek at them ... No conversing ... and still communicate!

You'll not only be a puzzler ... but a prize.

It'll be child's play ... yes ... go on ... be game.

Boyish and girlish qualities can have a beguiling effect. Even for the most stuffy and seemly.

Don't go overboard ... but you <u>can't</u> hook anyone with <u>one</u> line.

Picture a children's party ...

Self-propelling ... supersonic ... soaring ... always taking off ... never thinking of time ... other things ... or going into a tailspin.

Blasting ... yes!

But free and easy ... frank ... fun! And not so very formal!

Teenagers and others swayed by peer pressure are stuff and nonsense ...

Why is it "hip" ... "in" ... "with-it"?

Who is the peeeeer ... who reeled them in to be a parrot?

Just peeeer or patter right back.

By now ... you should be a genius at creating your own gems.

If you put into practice your <u>own</u> <u>potent</u> <u>personality</u> ... you might inspire others to stream ahead ... instead of being the same samples with dress ... drink ... deeds ... doings.

A college engaged me to shoot the breeze with students ... to do more activities within the school ... without alcohol.

At a Christmas celebration luncheon ... for the Salvation Army ... hundreds attended knowing alcohol was not allowed. Young people sang ... others told stories ... gave speeches ... and made splashes of other activity.

Not 90 proof, but 100% proof in the pudding that you are peer ... less!

By showing others ... you're a blast ... not a bust.

There was a sexy young man from Mars
Who enjoyed caviar and cigars at bars
He met a gal who was square
And found that he could care
So au revoir to the bizarres
Which weren't good for the glandulars ... anyhow.

Savvy ... sportive ... and spirited makes you soooo sexy!

Time to nip it in the bud!

If music be the food of love ... play on.
                                        —Shakespeare

Lorraine's Lively Liquids

Golden Margarita

1½ ounces tequila
¾ ounce Grand Marnier
2 ounces sour mix
pinch lime juice

Popular and peppy.

Than-Ah-Boor

Model amounts.

Cook ½ lb. pearl barley ... with a dash of salt in water to cover ... until well done ... about one hour.

In the meantime ...

Mix two quarts of plain yogurt or any fruit if desired ... with cold water ... beat well ... making buttermilk.

Thick ... thin ... up to you.

Refrigerate.

Drain barley thoroughly ... cool ... then add to buttermilk ... Mix ... chill.

Healthy and hearty.

Armenian Coffee

Serves 6 people.

1 brass Middle Eastern coffee pot
6 demitasse cups and saucers
Pulverized Armenian coffee
5 single packets sugar
cold water

Measure 5 cups of water with a demitasse cup.

For the sixth cup, add milk ... whole or skim ... instead of water and put all the liquid into the coffeepot.

Measure heaping ½ teaspoons of coffee 6 times ... and drop into water.

Add 5 packets of sugar and stir thoroughly.

Now stir occasionally ... put on high heat until it comes to a boil. Take it off the stove at once.

Put on heat ... <u>twice</u> more to a boil ... This is very ... very ... quick. Don't let it spill over.

Remove from stove.

With a spoon ... take foam from the top of the pot and drop into each cup and then pour coffee.

There are <u>many</u> versions of this Middle Eastern beverage.

This recipe is mine ... and received raves.

<u>"Fun" Fortune Telling</u>

When you finish the coffee ... turn the cup over ... Turn completely around three times ...

Place your palm on cup ... and make a wish.

When cup is cool ... turn it over ... If it sticks slightly to saucer ... your wish may come true.

Let someone else read your fortune ... and you read theirs.

Make it up ... make it funny ... but <u>no serious</u> sidelines.

The myths should be merry ... winning and warm.

Daddy's Delicious Delight

1 quart grape juice
3 quarts water
2 cups sugar
2 teaspoons citric acid
2 fresh oranges—squeezed
2 fresh lemons—squeezed
1 sliced orange for decoration
1 sliced lemon for decoration

Makes 2 pitchers of punch.

Chill ...

When serving drink in a punch bowl ... add colorful ice cubes ... of red ... orange ... yellow.

A punch he was proud of.

Be pleased as punch to play your part in ....

A Party Is Like a Play.

*"Now, don't go calling the sex police, or anything,
but I think you're swell."*

Chapter VII

A PARTY IS LIKE A PLAY

All the world's a stage, and all the men and women merely players. They have their exits and their entrances; and one in his time plays many parts.
—Shakespeare

And more entertaining for you and others.

By now ... you should be in the silver/gold stage.

Changing completely and continually! Don't stop—

You are confident of your rolls ... and are as smooth as butter. You realize now before you become a banquet ... you must be an appealing appetizer!

Oh ... you want to go over your script ... okay!

Action!!!

You are the star ... the celebrity ... Yes ... you are. Annnd—the writer ... producer ... director.

How did you create your characters? No! Never mind the others—yet! ... Your characters? And your many, many parts!

Go for a hair trim ... a face-lift ... diet pills ... and you can still be a pill.

Your rags are all the rage ... your makeup flawless ... but you still have flaws ...

Why? ... You tell me!

Maybe because you put faith in your façade ... rather than your Honesty ... Honor ... Humor!

Hmmmmm?

Are you stimulating ... secure and seasoned?

If you go ... go ... go ... they will go gaga over you.

You can count on it ... You won't need a calculator or computer to figure it out for you.

Add up your own assets.

It's a snap to shape forms and colors at your fingertips ... and acquire information on the Internet.

But what are you doing? Sitting ... Sitting ... Sitting ... You can't allow only that appliance to net you a ... game ... set ... match! You need to earn the points yourself.

Why ... oh ... why ... is it both genders beat their brains out to learn about schooling ... business ... sports ... or sprucing up ...

But sex ... piece of cake ... instant pudding ... let them stir me ... or crab ... crab ... crab.

If only you would remember that the right recipe is worth the wait ... and your party will always be a picnic ... because you shared ... served and gave an extra helping.

No more brass rings ... You're the silver lining ... and at the end of the rainbow ... the pot of gold ... just brewing for you!

Coach yourself <u>first</u> ... then go on <u>any</u> stage!

Don't think of your failings ... In fact ... <u>don't</u> <u>think</u> ... Perform ...

Don't sneer or snivel—

I'm not Scaramouch!

Ohhhhh ... nooooo?

Or *I'm shy ... I'm not a show-off.*

<u>No one</u> is shy ... just insecure ... and that is a form of conceit ... Everyone loves to show off <u>something</u> ... of theirs.

To be real ... you must be theatrical ...

If you both would only cast out chagrins and burst out with <u>sure</u> ... <u>grins</u>!

Faith ... hope ... charity ... but the greatest of these is trust.

<u>And</u> <u>tickling</u> <u>each</u> <u>other's</u> <u>funny</u> <u>bones</u>.

Change should be <u>in</u>spired an l <u>in</u>stigated. <u>Then</u> ... the <u>out</u>come and the <u>out</u>going.

Charrrrrge ... and you know I don't mean overcharge ... and pay later.

If you've rehearsed your role ... now cast the rest of the play.

Auditions!

You <u>are</u> a director.

It can be fatiguing or fun ... your pick ...

But you're prudent enough to separate the wheat from the chaff! And when you pick a "friend," don't peel that banana too soon.

There are countless ways to audition ... and one is <u>not</u> ... the casting couch.

When you've chosen the choicest ... make sure your script is well written. Scratch off ... revise and recast ... No scribbling or dashing off ...

When prepared ... get the show on the road ... but be sure when you do a road show out of town ... you don't travel out of your depth.

So you flubbed ... did a pratfall ... came in on a wrong cue ... <u>So</u> ... <u>what</u>! ... Make a comeback.

You will perform many exits and entrances ... hopefully with your best foot forward.

A steady run of good scenes and sincerity will result in good reviews ... There'll always be a critic who'll pan your portrayal ... and serve you one up better.

Rehearse ... rehearse ... rehearse ... backwards ... forwards ... inside ... then ... outward ... and you could <u>give</u> a command performance.

The art of speaking in a loud clear voice; and the avoidance of bumping into furniture.
>   —Alfred Lunt

Don't look at me, Sir, with—ah—in that tone of voice.
>   —Punch

You've milked other machines ... computer ... calculator ... copier ... fax ... VCR ... others ... Now ... bring into play ... the tape recorder. Read aloud the alphabet ... the Bible ... and Mother Goose ... and especially songs ...

Frank Sinatra ... Barbra Streisand ... Madonna ... all top vocalists ... enunciate everything ... and their tones top-notch.

You <u>are</u> a singer ... star ... second to none.

The heart of the fool is in his mouth, but the mouth of the wise man is in his heart.
>   —Benjamin Franklin

I don't mind your tongue being in your cheek, but I suspect your heart is there with it.
>   —Alan Bennett

Why ... oh why ... at every turn ... do family ... friends ... any flock ... finagle ... flimflam ... twist you around their finger ... toy with ... turn and twirl your words around so you're the one at fault?

You should at that golden stage ... strut your stuffing ... Show you're no turkey ... or you will lay an egg.

Sometimes ... be silent!

There is a time of speaking and a time of being still.

—William Caxton

Even a fool, when he holdeth his peace, is counted wise.

—The Bible

One great art of conversation.

—William Hazlitt

I must be silent, if I would be loved.

—Anna Wickham

Not a puppet ... pawn ... or like Punch and Judy ... but spicy ... sparkling ... and silent.

The only place where real truth is to be found.

—Pablo Picasso

One picture is worth more than a thousand words.

—Chinese proverb

As in cooking ... do you know how to mix and coat well ... or is your menu flat ... flavorless ... or too flashy?

Did you draw ... sketch ... wipe off and pencil in ... and outline your chef d'oeuvre?

Your scenes shouldn't be off-color ... or grow pale ... but flicker with freshness ... because you have a coat of many colors.

Paint the town red ... but if laid out in lavender ... or full of hot air ... those red balloons will carry you away.

Hip with zip!

Fashion is what one wears oneself. What is unfashionable is what other people wear.
                                        —Oscar Wilde

Not just clothes ... but customs ... conduct ... codes.

A sheep in sheep's clothing.
                                        —Winston Churchill

A sweet disorder in dress
kindles in clothes a wantonness.
                                        —Robert Herrick

When you've seen a nude infant doing a backward somersault, you know why clothing exists.

                                        —Stephen Fry

To have the best kind of fling
You might think you don't wear a thing.
But to add sweetening
To the festive evening
It's better to be featuring
A fashion flavored with zing.

To pull it over ... under wraps is winning and warming. And with a presentation.

It's chic to be current!

If you assume men and women don't pore over your attire ... colors ... nail polish ... fingernails ... hairstyle ... how trendy you are ... and distinct qualities ... you're back to your salad days.

Both genders notice <u>everything</u> ... <u>everything</u>! And <u>talk</u> about it!

Too much on the exterior ... and not the inner profile ... That's <u>wear</u> you both are off the mark.

What modish manner do you have?

Never mind if others are sloppy ... see-through ... stuffy ... stagnant ...

Any known ... local or national figure you admire ... never grew like Topsy ... They burst forward ... by <u>practice</u> ... <u>pains</u> ... and <u>proceeding</u> with a <u>plan</u> ... producing their own play.

The play's the thing ...
—Shakespeare

Too many use common clichés ... no creativity ... cobwebs ...

Or they set up shopworn ... sympathetic ploys ... gamey gimmicks ... the control craft.

If you are preeminent ... you wouldn't put up with that bidding.

Rehearse with other "actors" for your own repertoire.

There will be dozens of character changes ... sundry scenes ... and settings ... themes ...

But no matter where you roam
You know you'll always feel at <u>home</u>.

You ... he ... she ... "it" ... must take <u>part</u> ... to have a partner.

And don't forget the salt ... peppppper ... lines ... pantomime ... props ... music ... lighting ... budget ... playbill (invitations) ... audience ... co-directors — producers ... stars ... cast ... goodies ...

That curtain should never go up ... unless you repeatedly rehearse your characters ... scenes ... and rewrite the script.

<u>The</u> right recipe takes time ... training ... to be on the right track ... and catch the nonstop ... not the sleeper ... coach or Pullman.

There are many productions that were sleepers ... and became overnight expresses ...

Come on ... catch that choo-choo!

All aboard — the stage coaching is here.

You're acting all the time. Maybe as a bit player ... walk-on ... even the lead, but always that bright star that makes <u>others</u> shine.

Do one's part with props ... and not just cars ... credit cards ... computers.

A fan ... cane ... shawl ... feathers ... feather duster ... crazy chapeaus ... oranges ... and hairstyles ... veils ... Dutch shoes ... boots ... masks ... makeup. You can buy most of these items at costume shops. They are not expensive. A fan could cost less than $1.00. Make or borrow them. The music is in the library ... so are customs and costume books.

These items are more for women.

For you men ... romantic songs ... dramatic symphonies ... (you be the musical conductor) ... relating a fascinating book or play ... or wearing a sombrero and blanket ... you can both hide under.

Try numerous countries ... and be someone else. Express yourself in pantomime in a foreign "language" and ways. Create a skit ... situation or dance. No words. And do not be passive.

You could be a hot-blooded Italian actor who wants his way or <u>else</u>.

So many classic characters ... steps ... situations you can create.

But a million-dollar smile and sparkling eyes ... is the Midas touch.

Your drawing-room piece will not only be a drawing card ... but your profiles and pantomime will paint a prolific portrait.

Also ... what packs a punch ... is politeness ... and polish.

Don't you <u>dare</u> proclaim propriety is passé.

It's crucial in the chase.

You may be very, very lonely ... if you don't watch your p's and q's.

My version: prudence and quality.

Music expresses that which cannot be said and on which it is impossible to be silent.

—Victor Hugo

The universal language of mankind.

—Henry Wadsworth Longfellow

Music is a higher revelation than philosophy.

—Ludwig Van Beethoven

The speech of angels.

—Thomas Carlyle

Only you can compose your own concert ... set the tone ... rhythm ... harmony ... sounds ... adagio ... andante.

But if you wing it ... too brassy ... stringing along ...

Music helps not the toothache.

—George Herbert

Music should be major ... not minor.

And what tune ... told you ... to use standard lightbulbs?

I pointed out that at my party, I dressed up my décor with multicolored lights.

What a fantastic feature! A finishing touch and turn-on ... Try it.

Being a star ... presenting soirées ... being fashionable ... with all its fun ... <u>could</u> cost a pretty penny.

But if you buy two colored bulbs ... a 39¢ fan or orange ... music cassette or disc from the library ... coffee ... donuts ... you can lick by ... with your prize pick and you as a prize package ... You can't miss.

Different dishes ... assorted stemware ... classical with contemporary furniture ... diverse décor ... are correct ... as long as the accessories accent your adornment.

Too firm and formal ... doesn't furnish fascination.

A "perfect" party is passionless and pointless.

I don't mean a dramatic disaster ... but a foul-up could be funny and not forgotten.

There are <u>no</u> rules ... except decency and decorum ... Oh, yes ... being a bit of a lark who laughs.

Instigate an invitation of your own invention ... by hand ... computer ... or whatever.

Any invitation for any production ... social ... professional ... fund-raising ... should always <u>reveal</u> ... you ... tempting ... tangy ... tantalizing.

What a standout ... showing who you are ... what you're going to present.

Expose ... display ... out-dazzle ... out-glitter ... upstage ... them all.

Your gig ... will be <u>the</u> most glamorous ... grandstand ... gala ... they've every attended.

The event does <u>not</u> need to be expensive ... just <u>expressive</u>!

Too much flash ... could be a crashing bore.

<u>Telephoning</u> ... are you gung-ho ... happy ... or does the other person wish they could hang up?

Be that way ... Be upbeat even when you beg the plumber to fix the faucet ... right away ... or try to acquire a loan.

Sometimes it is good to be gritty ... plucky ... severe ... but sense <u>when</u> you can pull those strings.

Show business! ... You see ... you're constantly on a soapbox, treading the boards in several scenes ... in singular situations.

Confident ... charming ... coltish ...

Even when things are topsy-turvy ... here ... there ... everywhere ... you must deliver ... Otherwise ... you'll be pulled by Bo Peep's staff off the stage.

There are a number of pieces you can run through ... catch phrases ... and I don't mean ...

Have a nice day ... is as plausible as a puppet on a string.

'Are you playing games with me?' ... with my above-it-all air ... always gets them ... no matter who it is ... or what incident.

Again ... and ... again ... <u>do</u> <u>your</u> <u>own</u> <u>thing</u>.

Also ... a reminder ... It's not what you <u>say</u> ... that counts.

Keep a storage of significant signs and sayings that are <u>your</u> signature ... whether ... personal or professional.

Your career is constantly with you ... no matter what ground you cover ... personally or professionally.

Sometimes you may be just a part of a play.

You can still be a VIP if you go along with the setting ... to be or not to be ... sparkling or silent.

Your star should guide you in giving situations.

So launch your own lines that are clever ... captivating ... and you'll cruise on a luxury <u>liner</u>!

And those close to your heart ... compose ... confide ... with <u>secret</u> <u>signals</u> ... that are inventive ... inviting.

Speaking of stars ... there is always one that is more sparkling than others ... and yet ... they are all still consolidated ... collectively in the solar system.

Remember ... the right recipe or meal ... has many multitudes.

Even a hotdog is enhanced with mustard ... relish ... onions ... dripping with sauerkraut ... pouring on the ketchup ... with a sesame seed bun.

Your favorite frosting is ringing in ... or rooms with you ... Never lay the icing on too thick ... too perfectly ... or try to top or topple the topping.

Keep in mind ... they're in your play ... they support you ...
And in many ways ... they have a script of their <u>own</u>!

Men shrink from shopping ... though ... but not if you trump
your ace with treats.

Usually they don't mind ... going to the market ... especially
... if they have their own cart ... and pick their own lollipops!
Food ... that is ... food!

You both have a list and are checking it twice ...
Tasting the tacos with too much spice.
Each takes a cart ... bumps into the other ...
Squeezing ... the melon together ...
Discussing serving dirty rice ...
Rubbing a cherry ... and tossing it in their mouth.
No wonder you're both hungry and thirsty.
By the time you check out ... you're ready to check in.

You don't need any prompting or stage directions ... All the
places are clearly marked and mounted.

Just stay within the framework. If you stray from the
production ... and go into someone else's theater and do
their play ... (stepping on toes ... or being mean ...) that's
called plagiarism.

But if your backdrop doesn't quite touch the floor ... you
can't get it off the ground ... or it doesn't hang right ...
remember, no "play" or setting is perfect.

But don't ever ... ever ... ever ... be an understudy ...

These added suggestions to your script ... could be with a
couple or complete cast ...

<u>A</u> <u>party</u> <u>is</u> <u>like</u> <u>a</u> <u>play</u>!

Let's review!

*A bad review may spoil your breakfast, but you shouldn't
allow it to spoil your lunch.*
                                        —Kingsley Amis

First ... foremost ... forever ...

There's no better critic than <u>you</u>!

You ... you ... you ...

*Basic research is what I am doing when I don't know what I
am doing.*
                                        —Werner Von Braun

An investment in knowledge pays the best interest.

                                        —Benjamin Franklin

They know enough who know how to learn.

                                        —Henry Adams

*The struggling for knowledge hath a pleasure in it like that
of wrestling with a fine woman.*
                                        —Marquis of Halifax

Know thyself.
                                        —Plutarch

Picture yourself as your greatest fan ... with fanfare ... who
doesn't fantasize ... and is not <u>single</u>-minded.

And give your gift to others.

Then ... and only then ... will you acquire prestige ... popularity favor ... be positive ... polished ... features that are first rate ... for a first run ... in which you play many ... many parts.

I have a friend who didn't crack a smile or a joke ... when I met him. Who brought out his tee (terrific) <u>hee</u> side ... and now outdoes me with his repartee and repertoire.

You, too, can be remarkable ... if you radiate.

Your character will constantly change ... and will keep on changing for the <u>good</u>!

Of courrrrrse ... your exterior makeup will help "make" you over ... with ...

Fashion (which covers several scenes, not just clothes) ... pantomime ... voice ... manners ... skills ... whimsy ... parading your posture and funny feelings.

If you don't show or spread "it" ... you can stay <u>at</u> home instead of <u>being</u> at home.

Externally ... you may appear peerless ... and you may "<u>act</u>" the perfect part outside ...

But inside ... is more influential ... where you alone ... rule the roost.

<u>Home</u> ... at last!

And it's impossible ... impossible ... impossible ... to think you're homely or not good enough.

I said <u>not</u> to <u>think</u>!

You <u>are</u> ......

The master or mistress of ceremonies ... with congeniality ... creativity ... and, oh yes ... a clown!

Why fantasize and wish you could be someone else ...

When you can have flair ... power ... punch ... to be several <u>selves</u>!

Get through it ... Get by it ... Get with it ... Got "it"?

Anxious ... no ... Alluring ... yes.

Not deluxe ...

Deloooooooxe.

Remember all the preparations of a good meal.

The way to a man or woman's stomach ... is through <u>your</u> heart.

Life is too short to stuff a mushroom.
                                                    —Shirley Conran

And don't stuff yourself with building blocks.

You may not be a peachy pear ... so what!

Just don't be a sour grape.

Then you'll be caring ... believable ... loved ... and have top billing ...

The notion, years back ... that a man had to be introduced to the woman ... and a woman never made the first move ...

Move to the millennium. Advance ... charge ... jet ...

Or play second fiddle and sit out in the lobby alone.

We still engage in games and sports ... flooded with feigning ... finagling ... and no fair play.

Then a meteor emerges ... who is <u>square</u> ... but <u>sensational</u> ... with all the magic ... melody and sizzle.

Yes ... Virginia ... you can be square ... and still sizzle!!

Victor, too!

You could feature a new fad ... Fast is out ... finesse is in ...

Frustration is out ... faith is in ... your<u>selves</u>!

All the seats are filled with your feelings and for others.

There will be intermissions ... but mostly ...

You're a sellout!

Your magnetism ... drawing power ... is <u>the</u> main attraction.

Though there might be a *method in your madness* ... if on the marquee you had another principal player alongside of you.

Two principals in the cast can be a smash!

Hmmmmm??

No matter ... whether you only have a skit or synopsis ... As long as your features are firm ... fly with it.

They'll treasure you more if <u>both</u> of you are the toast of the town.

Take the bows ... hand in hand ... side by side ... cheek to cheek ... kissy and kissy and kissy and kissy and ... and ... and ...

The most suave ... hip ... swinging ... make it happen! And <u>now</u> <u>you're</u> <u>one</u> <u>of</u> <u>them</u>.

Surprise ... put on your shows of shows ... and you'll earn applause after applause.

And with your beau ... arm in arm ... rubbing ... elbows ... you can grin and bare it ... er ... bear it.

Classic clichés are commonplace.

Any Silly Billy ... Crabby Abby ... can ask ...

Would you like to come in for a cup of coffee?

With <u>that</u> ... they must think you're the <u>salt</u> of the earth ...

Anyone who presents that phrase ... or anyone who accepts it ... should ... Never mind ... just read my book ... 17 times!

They're like a satellite that orbits round and round ... not <u>landing</u> anywhere ... a pie in the sky ... instead of a star.

Jet away ... not fly-by-night ...

Spread out in space ... not spaced out ...

Soak up the atmosphere ... and don't get soaked.

Concentrate on circles ... that are delicious desserts.

No matter where you are seated in the theater ... you'll always appear to be in the ... dress circle ... because you're cool ... charming and confident ...

In the balcony ... you're above it all ... the seats squeeze closer together ... So do you ... if you're smart.

So no more cups of coffee ... too much of a bad habit. And you don't have to be rolling in dough ... to be rich in flavor.

With your new wardrobe change ... your wit ... hot off the griddle ... and way-out wooing words ... whoopee!

Build your own repertoire ... every situation is singular.

When saying "goodnight" ... Being coy is tooooo "cute" ... Being smug isn't smart ... Pulling a fast one ... is foolish.

If they take off ... never to come back to the tide ... it's <u>your</u> fault ... yes ... <u>yours</u>!

If you stimulated them in some other stagy way ... and fashioned a bit of showbiz ... concerning <u>them</u> ... there would be no farewells forever.

It's <u>true</u> ... <u>true</u> ... <u>true</u> ...

But <u>you</u> must be true ... even when you're theatrical!

Paradox? ... Nooooo!

Playing with pizzazz!

Mush ... to the millennium.

If you want to be rubbed the right way ... use elbow grease with flavor and flair.

<u>Women</u>:
How about dessert? It just needs to be heated up!

Then snatch his tie or jacket and push him in the kitchen.

I don't give a fig what other rules there are ...

Men adore being "ordered" and for women to take the lead ... but with femininity.

<u>Men</u>:
Do you have anything that needs fixing?

Rush for your toolbox ... and hold it up high.

If she doesn't have anything ... she'll find something ... if she has anything going for her.

Come on ... tap dance to your own tune ... You can ... do it on <u>your</u> <u>own</u>.

Use more than one recipe and <u>cook</u>book.

<u>Lorraine's</u> <u>Lucrative</u> <u>Ludicrous</u> <u>Looks</u>

For parties ... picnics ... public (social ... charitable ... business ... etc.) ... or private productions.

Fantasy and fact ... They can be on the same platform ... if you're up front ... and fun.

Your lead role ... will inspire others to take a principal part.

Themes with a twist!

Some of my favorites:

1. A French café or cabaret ... in Paris ... Ooooooh ...
   la la!

Food ... accents ... décor ... flags ... posters ... small intimate tables ... music ... songs ... dance ... but not too daring ... well ... why not?

Speak in French when you can't think of the English for a thing.
                                        —Lewis Carroll

2. Any foreign country and its flavor ... especially
   yours or theirs.

3. Acting like a mannequin or a wind-up doll.

At home ... pretend you're at ... a circus ... department store ... ballet ... you're someone's present ... and do their bidding ... or almost!

4. Don't speak one word ... all in pantomime ... body
   language (terrific in personal or professional
   presentations) ...

5. Entertain those who can't do it for themselves.

Nursing homes ... hospitals ... children in need of care want a few laughs, too. Spur your special to go with you.

The museum ... let me have cute harlequin dolls ... for 25¢. I bought hundreds ... and went to children's hospitals ... nursing homes ... to strangers who were in wheelchairs on the street and in malls ...

Once ... parents were wheeling their son ... I parked illegally ... and ran after them with my doll. They were so happy ... I will never forget the tears in the Father's eyes. It reminded me of my Father's ... when my sister passed away. One glad ... one sad ... but both heartwarming.

Do you want a bowl of cherries ... or the pits? ... It's your "play."

6. Wear a mesmeric mask ... as the only prop you have ... I did say the only <u>prop</u>.

If others want to wear one ... okay ... or just you ... It's your play.

7. Wear a zany wig or crazy costume.

8. Be a belly dancer ... (There <u>are</u> male belly dancers) ... clown ... glamorous doll ... whatever ...

9. Appear ... like a jet-setter ... reeking with wealth ... and savoir-faire.

A rich man is nothing but a poor man with money.

—W.C. Fields

Highbrow — the kind of person who looks at a sausage and thinks of Picasso.

—A.P. Herbert

10. A cartoon character ... spy/detective ... mystery author ... chef ... ghost ... séance medium ... cruise ship host ... fairy tale character ... circus ... cowboy or rock singer ... fashion model ... magician ... pirate ... you name it ...

Not a judo/karate expert ... breakage and sweaty.

A film ... TV ... theater ... opera ... ballet ... musical ... figure.

Contemporary or classic ... a celebrity.

11. Court another era ... 1920s ... 1890s ... space age ... the time is yours.

12. Think Carmen Miranda or Desi Arnaz ... with music ...

Place a fruit ... tray ... bowl ... wastebasket ... on your head ... or hip ... or wherever ... and roll everything ... especially your eyes ...

And feed the audience or that special one ... with grapes and yi yi yi or babaloo!

13. You could be major by hamming it up as a minor ... or tiny tot ... with duds ... balloons ... pin the tail on the donkey ... etc.

14. Conduct a symphony ... with a long wooden spoon ... and spoonerisms ... The food is your orchestra. It plays when and where you tell it. Accompanied by solos from pots ... counters ... glasses ... dishes ... Dish it up ...

15. Sports ... I don't have to tell you ...

16. Hobbies ... ditto!

Because — ?

Royalty ... regal ... refined ... is ranked as a gold winner.

<u>Baby</u> ... <u>take</u> <u>a</u> <u>bow</u>!

And how! Then "make" ....

Every Day a Holiday

Chapter VIII

EVERY DAY IS A HOLIDAY!

To everything there is a season, and a time to every purpose under the Heaven.
                                    —The Bible

Will you, won't you, will you, won't you, will you join the dance?
                                    —Lewis Carroll

A holiday can be honeyed up ... or goosed down ... It's up to you!

You wake up ... brush your teeth ... dress ... eat, etc. ... do personal/professional chores ... which you either crab ... crow ... or chuckle.

By now ... you can't help but chuckle ... chant ... cavort ... more.

A merrier hour was never wasted there.
                                    —Shakespeare

Sure there are pressures ... problems ... doubts ... headaches ... breakups ... arguments ... disappointments ... and on and on ...

Without exception ... they will exist.

Outstrip them all ...

It takes time ... but time will tell ... that you're ticklish and tender.

Yes, you men ... too! The prime filet is always tender ... and tickles the taste buds.

Pour it on ... beat the blues ... and whisk your worries away.

Don't let it get to you ... <u>you</u> get <u>it</u> ... to tumble into a turmoil and turn about.

Irritations into irresistibles!

Life is just one damned thing after another.

—Elbert Hubbard

Live ... live ... live ...
—Patrick Dennis

Are you going to charge or pay through the nose ... and be on loan the rest of your life?

Duty is what one expects from others. It is not what one does oneself.
—Oscar Wilde

You know everybody is ignorant, only on different subjects.

—Will Rogers

Look, he's winding up the watch of his wit, by and by it will strike.
—Shakespeare

To be striking, you must hit a bull's-eye ... most of the time ... or time will strike back.

Nearly all take a Sunday drive with their lives ... or cope and criticize with the Monday blues ... constantly.

But if you entertain everyday ... the end result will be elation ... rapture ... enthusiasm ...

Are you festive with those in a hospital ... or at a funeral?

Yes!!! Do!!! It will sustain and support them!

Naturally ... there are steps ... spans ... values that vary.

Only ... when necessary do I send flowers during those occasions.

With the nurse's permission ... I bring ice cream ... cake ... other goodies ... board games ... hand puppets ... and most of all ... cheer!

Homemade dishes delight those who are in mourning ... or go to a quiet restaurant ... to lift their spirits.

So you see ... everyday is a holiday ... when done in stages ... with scenes ... with a well-written script or skit.

It is better to have written a damned play, than no play at all—it snatches a man obscurity.
> —Frederic Reynolds

Women, too!

Toss your coin with warmth and well-wishing ... instead in the wishing well.

Go ahead, be wishy-washy ... and wash your wishes down the drain.

If a man could have half his wishes ... he would double his troubles.
                                        —Benjamin Franklin

We do not succeed in changing things according to our desires, but gradually our desire changes.

                                        —Marcel Proust

Because you <u>do</u> or <u>don't</u>!

<u>Hundreds</u> ... <u>thousands</u> ... no matter what age ... just <u>wait</u> for <u>others</u> to turn them on.

They're stale ... no spark ... stagnant ... sitters ... complainers ... confused ... or they're loose as a goose ... and blame everyone except themselves!

Even those at the top of the ladder are frustrated ... naive ... testy ... dreamers ... babyish ... vapid ... vain ... vulnerable.

Entertainment ... entertainment ... entertainment!!!

I'm bored with ...

Women! *"All the good men are taken"* ... *"How did <u>she</u> get him?" "If it happens it happens."*

Grrrrr!!

Men:

"All they want is a career or money and not me." "How do I get out of this bad scene?"

<u>You</u> wrote <u>and</u> <u>directed</u> the play!!

There is only one thing in the world worse than being talked about, and that is not being talked about.

—Oscar Wilde

Others may be milk ... masquerading as cream ... and hope that it's healthier for them ... especially if it's skim ... or homogenized.

They can have a bland life ... they are backstage ... instead of in front of the footlights ... grumble ... gossip ... but not take a moment to modernize or elevate themselves.

You have dished me up, like a savoury omelette, to gratify the appetite of the reading rabble for gossip.

—Thomas Love Peacock

I'm called away by particular business—but I leave my character behind me.
—Richard Brinsley Sheridan

What is <u>your</u> appraised value? Not worth a plug nickel if you won't <u>put in</u> your two cents' worth.

But why on earth am I asking you these ˅apid questions?

You're no longer an art object ... curio ... or curiosity piece ... wasting away on the shelf full of dust.

Are <u>you</u>?

No way ... You've been nominated for an award for your portrayal of the man/woman of a thousand faces.

Just be sure it isn't a false front ... er ... disguise ... It's really you ... and you ... and you ... and ...

Are you that fortunate cookie that doesn't get crumbled ... unless you want to?

Who took the squeeze out of the lemon ... and squashed all the blueberries and crab apples ... then scooped up a decadent dessert of sundae à la mode?

Every day!

That's right ... no more guessing ... off the cuff ... sudden ... stupid ... stirrings. It's yum ... yum ... yummy <u>you</u>!

How can anyone resist you?

You've got "it" ... with all the tempting toppings.

They want to order from your menu.

With flair ... flavors ... fiestas ...

It's not what you serve ... but <u>how</u> you serve "it" up.

If they're naggy ... namby-pamby ... nasty ... tell them they're out of order ... and tilt them in another direction.

Don't <u>say</u> things. What you <u>are</u> stands over you the while, and thunders so that I cannot hear what you say to the contrary.

—Emerson

There is nothing in this world constant, but inconstancy.

—Jonathan Swift

'Tis strange — but true; for truth is always strange; stranger than fiction.

—Lord Byron

His wit invites you by his looks to come, but when you knock, it is never at home.

—William Cowper

Women, too!

If you were in a theatrical production ... you wouldn't dare attempt to act without rehearsals ... knowing the script ... characters and lines.

Why wing it in actual affairs.

Day in and day out ... don't forget afternoons and evenings ... you're ... <u>at</u> <u>home</u> ... <u>no</u> <u>matter</u> <u>where</u> <u>you</u> <u>are</u>.

A sportive emcee ... who enjoys spreading ecstasy.

Let's digest once more. To meet ... to mushroom ... to cut the mustard ... requires <u>scores</u> of right recipes ... and not to sit or stand ... but to stir.

I thought one fellow didn't stir me ... a turkey.

My mother ... said ... *He must be smart ... if he's an attorney.*

'I don't care ... he's still a drip.' Was I all wet ... wow!

How did I know he was fantastic? ... By being with him ... and doing a project together.

Be a <u>greeter</u> at church or synagogue. It worked for me ... and for others I encouraged ... (men and women). If they don't have a group ...

<u>Start</u> <u>something</u>!!

Also ... committees ... fundraisers ... theatre ... all as a team. This should always be at the tip of your tongue ... no matter what position (in looks or in life), you are on stage at all times ... never backstage.

So many strongly relate they will join ... but let someone else start it. If they feel that strongly ... why don't they put that energy to steam or simmer ... for a mouth-watering menu?

Suppose there is a drop from the clouds ... you shower it with a savoir-faire surprise and sunshades.

Sunshades will not block the sun ... but screen you from the rays or rose-colored ruses.

Besides ... it magnifies a bit of mystery.

Flow with the tide together ... Instead of them being the sand in your shoe. They could be the golden slipper ... if <u>you</u> fit it faithfully.

If your "friends" ... focus or forecast on ...

I hate to spread rumours, but what else can one do with them?
—Amanda Lear

At your formal soirée, they wear dungarees ... are ultra-late or gross ... soil your sofa ... or hit on or drop your favorite dish ...

What to do ... what to do ...

This is one time you <u>do</u> <u>nothing</u> ... just smile ... snicker ... shrug ... but <u>never</u> sneer or "say" anything.

Better to keep your mouth shut and appear stupid than to open it and remove all doubt.
—Mark Twain

<u>To</u> <u>yourself</u>:

No second banana is going to upstage me ... total my tryout ... ruin my repertory company and troupe on me! No way!

Bear it all with boxing gloves ... <u>silently</u> ... showing them with body language.

Or wear a kimono with kid gloves ... drape yourself ... be dramatic ... darling and delightful!

When young kids kick up a ruckus ... they usually don't carry a grudge ... gripe ... or are full of grief.

Grown-ups ... fortify that yoke and yeast for years ... whereas the child is automatic ... nonchalant ... accepting naturally ... being happy-go-lucky. You need

<u>happy</u> and <u>go</u> ... but ... <u>luck</u> ... is like a colander ... It doesn't hold water ... too many holes ... that could drain you.

But have your "holidays" hold fast ... and form your hallmark.

We all recognize the regular ... reputable days.

Standard ones ... should be extra special ... Every day should be super-duper, too!

Why wait for well-known holidays ... How about the unwritten ones?

St. Cupid's Day ... Hanky-Panky Day ... No Hanky-Panky Day ... Bunny Hop Day ... Single's Birthday ...

Dessert Day ... Apple Dumpling Day ... Second Helping Holiday ... Sugar and Spice Occasion ... Crusty Bun Celebration ...

Hot Tamale Day ... Leftover's Birthday ... Sticky Syrup's Birthday ... Peel Me a Grape Day ... Honey Yam's Birthday ... Pickled Peach's Birthday ...

Golden Goose Day ... Candied Cherry's Birthday ... Cherry and Cheery Day ... Hot Fudge Day ... Tart's Birthday ... Field Day ...

Makeup Day

Make "It" Celebration

Make One Up Day

Just Out of the Hospital Holiday

Gals:

New Lipstick Day ...

Just bought a new color ... want you to try it out.

Guys:

New Toy Day ...

Just bought ... don't say what ....

Everybody's Birthday Party ... all signs ... of the spectrum ... on cake ... food ... décor ...

Anybody who has a birthday can come ... those you and your friends know ... that is. Never a free-for-all.

What is your feast day? Bet yours is better ... and packed with more punch!

Never "familiar" ... unrefined ... flat ... or it will be the fall of the curtain on the last act.

Hoopla your holidays to the hilt ...

Whoop-de-do ... fun ... not frenzied or wild.

Play your key note!

A thoughtful touch ... nicknames ...

Helps to put the show on the road ... to become closer ... confident ... confidential ... personal ... palsy-walsy ... close to one's heart ...

<u>Possible</u> <u>pet</u> <u>names</u>:

Bunny ... rabbit ... bow-<u>wow</u> ... meow ... purrrrrydy ... tootsie ... sugar plum ... ginger snap ... snickers ... poopsie ... popsie ... da da ... ga ga ... ha ha ... numero uno ... mama mia ... bitsy-witsy ... foo-foo ... twinkle toes ... cutesy ... wootsey ... cuddly-winks ... winkie poo ...

It doesn't matter how sophisticated or simple they are ... they adore ... appreciate ... appetizing perky perts.

But don't do "it" ... without doing you ... first!

<u>If</u> you yourself know you are <u>the</u> kitten or tomcat's meow,

And if you love with a purpose ... you'll be purrrrrfect.

Added ingredients:

True friendship ... never a falsehood ... fun ... funny!

Sift ... shift ... stir ... snappy ...

To be sexy ... sexier ... sexiest ...

Women must be cool to be hot ...

Men must be hot to be cool.

Looks have nothing ... absolutely nothing ... nothing ... nothing ... nothing ... to do with "it"!

<u>Looks</u> ... but not being a sight ... sloppy ... sly ... slick ... sticky ...

Otherwise ... call it a day ... and your hay and holidays ... will be a haystack of straw.

Men and women ... both ... question ...

What can I do to catch them?

I never can meet the kind I want.

Why can't I get to first base?

Why do <u>they</u> treat me that way? What did <u>I</u> do?

Why can't I get them to notice me?

Where are they?

<u>I'll</u> <u>tell</u> <u>you</u> <u>where</u> <u>to</u> <u>go</u> ...

<u>Lorraine's</u> <u>Lucid</u> <u>Locations</u>

<u>Stock</u> <u>Scenes</u>

Church/synagogue	Friends
Family	Parties
Market	Travel
Conventions/associations/ meetings	Business Chance meetings
Charities	Political gatherings
Restaurants	Magazines/newspaper ads
Shopping	Beauty salon
Beach	Exercise club
Sports club/sporting events	Singles clubs

<u>Anywhere</u>!!!

<u>It</u> <u>isn't</u> <u>where</u> … <u>but</u> <u>what</u> … <u>you</u> <u>do</u>!

You can't <u>want</u> or <u>wait</u>

<u>Work</u> it out <u>yourself</u> … now!

<u>Lorraine's</u> <u>Own</u> <u>Box</u> <u>Office</u> <u>Hits</u>

1. <u>Play</u>: Your own production … pull one off …

   a. Church/synagogue
   b. Charity
   c. Friends/family
   d. Parties
   e. Singles groups
   f. Dozens of others

Choose a contemporary piece and purchase … (not expensive) … the play at a place like Samuel French, Inc., in New York.

Find a home … condo … hall … (for free) and cast and crew pool costs. You'd be amazed how many want to jump in the pool … either for fun or fundraising.

"Order" everyone around. They'll love every minute of it … because it's polished off with finesse … flair … flavor …

And not only is the production a hot item … but guess <u>who</u> else is??

And it's up to you to make <u>them</u> ... especially your main feature ... feel fabulous and far out.

Do you recall my original skit ... when several suave ... sexy men rehearsed with me ... just for entertainment and enjoyment?

That was ten years ago ... and they're all still my friends.

The scenario ...

Men and women ... you now know your onions ... Create your own concoction. But you <u>won't</u> <u>click</u> with clichés!

2. <u>Political</u>: Remember when I was in the mood to meet a special man ... I sure did!

I coined a committee for a big boffo boat cruise.

And asked all around the mulberry bush ... cutting that mustard ... for men ... to be on my committee!

Please don't ask <u>if</u> I had success ... <u>know</u>!

The candidate's colors were green and blue ... so when we had a meeting at my home ... guess what?

Green and blue lights ... decor ... plus pistachio pudding ... blue cheese ... blueberry pie ... green grapes ... and so on ...

3. <u>Singles</u> <u>Groups</u>: Was on the social singles' team at my church.

What a wonderful way to meet men ... and what terrific times we had.

We went everywhere ... private homes, condos ... beach ... concerts ... museums ... polo matches ... boat trips ... dances ... <u>you</u> name it.

Church/synagogue events aren't ho-hum ... stuffy ... or high-hat ... just the opposite ... plus marvy men and women.

Other singles clubs have sprouted throughout the world ... and most are refined ... well organized ... meet at respectable places ... and are very with-it.

There are a few "private" ones ... but <u>still</u> on the up-and-up. You must be invited. If you inspire ... you will be.

One Valentine's evening, a fellow friend clued me in about this group having a gathering at a large private home. About 130 to 150 people came ... didn't know one gal there ... and just three male acquaintances.

So singles are out there ...

You've got to be out to be in and in to be out.

If that makes sense ... you'll be a sensation!

    4. <u>Parties</u>: Toss away the book ... You now have the total look that can throw anyone ...

You're tip-top ... <u>the</u> toast of the town who struts his/her stuff ... go for "it."

The golden way
<u>Is</u> a soirée.

Not only are you on home ground ... but you write your own ticket ... and everyone has to board your ship.

Give them a festive time they'll never forget.

People remember my parties ... that were produced ... several years ago ... They recall even the fine points ...

Never ... sit ... chat ... stand ... crunch ...

Every moment is on the move ... They'll be caught in the act.

A play ... that has the cast craving to be in your next production ... no matter where it is.

 5. Play games: Don't be a sport ...

If you look it up ... synonyms are ... laughingstock ... everybody's fool ... goat ... schnook ... sitting duck ... soft mark ...

Instead ... be sportive ... playful ... full of fun ... cheerful ... spirited ... coltish ... kittenish ... debonair ...

 6. Beach/travel: What a way to be in the swim of
      things ... and to perceive a person's personality.

Casual ... relaxed ... back to back ... rubbing sunscreen and/or elbows with each other.

Everyone's essence is exposed.

You're fashionable ... figure things out ... and realize your figure and face aren't the main factors ... but your unmatched features ... and what you can offer.

If you're at the "rehearsal" stage ... (not steady or married) ... men and women rent a summer place ... or go on a romantic, friendly junket ... wherever you like.

Terms: Dutch treat ... annnnd ...

No hanky-panky!

Annnnnnd ... stick to it!

Guaranteed: You'll find more friends and make new friends ... who would want to be a party to it ... for that is what it would be.

It works ... it works ... it works ... wonders!

No more cutesy ... crabby ... coyness ... cutting ... clichés ... calculating ...

On anyone's part!

You refuse to allow it!!

By being genuine ... gregarious ... giving ... "good" ... you'd be amazed how others will bounce on your bandwagon.

The music ... method ... mode ... manners ... are yours ...

This is the Jet Age ... move to the millennium ... Zing ... zoom ... zip ... into action.

Never act silly or be standard again ... because you are skilled in any situation.

Your personality is so paramount ... people will perceive you as a star.

Not only <u>are</u> <u>you</u> …

But you treat others … as someone special, too!

<u>There's</u> <u>the</u> <u>secret</u> <u>ingredient</u>!

<u>Now</u> <u>cook</u> <u>up</u> <u>a</u> <u>storm</u>!!!

SMELL THE AROMA OF AMOUR … AUJOURD'HUI!

The Beginning!

"Are you unhappy, Darling?"
"Oh, yes, yes! Completely."

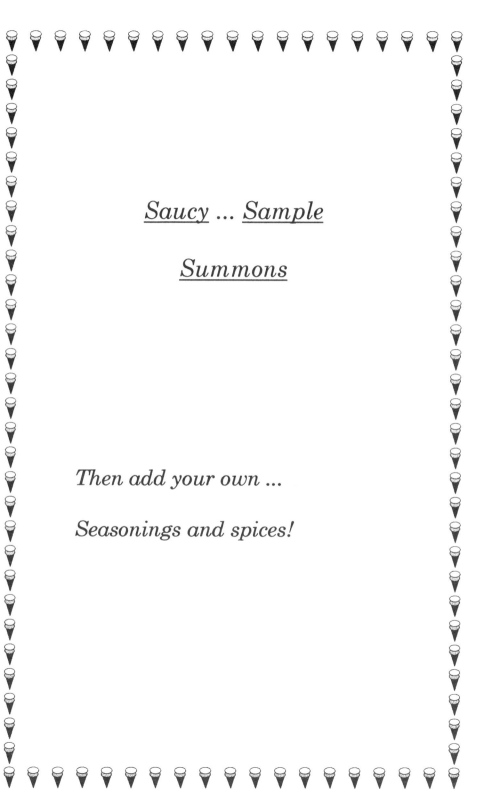

Saucy ... Sample

Summons

Then add your own ...

Seasonings and spices!

You're invited to:

"Sexy Food for Singles" Soirée

<u>Place</u>:   (Use your imagination)

<u>Date</u>:   (Whatever)

<u>Time</u>:   (Be unique)

<u>Meeeee</u>:

R.S.V.P.

Aye to I

<u>Sundae à la Mode</u>

I scream for you to ...

Make "it" on your own ...

<u>Dip in at</u>:   Time _____

<u>Sprinkling</u>:   ___   Place   ___

<u>Nuts</u> ... er ... <u>Date</u> _____

Topped by that ... cherry

With bing ... o ... solo ... mio!

<u>Show</u> <u>Up</u> <u>and</u> <u>Show</u> <u>Off</u>

Carmen or Carmen Miranda

Hamlet or just a ham

Show at _____ Place _____

Showtime _____

Show business produced by _____

_____

Mix and Stir

Punch in or roll in

With your goods and ... "goodies"

Check in: _____ Date _____

Clock in: _____ Time _____

Inside: _____ Place _____

Invited by: _____

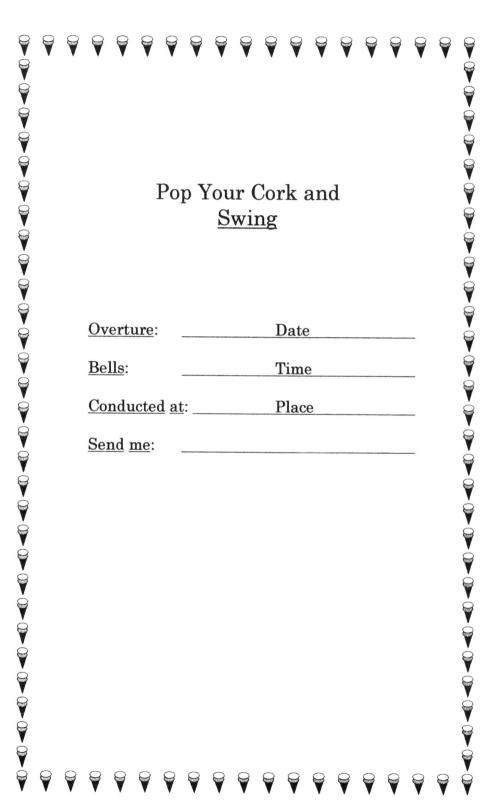

Pop Your Cork and
<u>Swing</u>

<u>Overture</u>:   _____ Date _____

<u>Bells</u>:   _____ Time _____

<u>Conducted at</u>:   _____ Place _____

<u>Send me</u>:   _____

Come over ... and ...

COOK UP A STORM

I'm ready ...

For that right recipe ...

<u>You</u>!!!

I HAVE NOTHING TO WEAR

Phil called. He suggested romance.
He cooed, "Let's go out and dance."

I was in love, I was in a trance.
This calls for a new outfit, I thought, that I can't finance.
For I need desperately my body to enhance
Due to my overindulgence and my rear end's expanse.

But, even with my plastic
There wasn't a chance.
So to my closet I did advance.
I opened the doors and took a glance.

Will it be my blond chiffon, my grape crêpe, or my
tangerine sateen?
Maybe my austere cashmere, my café chambray, or my
new ultramarine gabardine?
Possibly my gray moiré, my green crêpe de chine,
Or even my aquamarine velveteen…?

Nothing looked right. Everything I tried, a fright.
Oh God. Why wasn't I born slight?
They were all just a little too tight.
Even my white dress that was downright dynamite.

Clothes were strewn on the floor
And piled on the bed.
I know!
My new outfit in that yummy shade of red!

Deeper into my closet I did ransack.
Maybe my black, with the daring bare back,
Or my lilac sacque
Trimmed in cognac?

I give up!

All I could do was stare in despair.
All my outfits were so très ordinaire.
I simply cannot go out anywhere
For I have absolutely nothing to wear!

I swear, I swear,
I will never eat another chocolate éclair.

I know! I'll bathe and shampoo my hair.
Spray perfume everywhere...
Get a little champagne and camembert
Out of the Frigidaire.

A little dinner I'll prepare: filet mignon,
Nice and juicy and rare.
For dessert, chocolate sauce over poached pear.
Phil had better beware.

He's a millionaire,
The one I am determined to ensnare...
I want that diamond solitaire
So, I'll just entertain him in my underwear.

Poor Phil doesn't have a prayer.

Hmmmmm...Let's see. I think it will be
My pink, slink, bikini pants from France
With my café au lait, appliqué negligée...
S'il vous plâit.

Want More?

Books ... Books ... Books ...
With Ten (10) New Yorker Cartoons

Call: 1-877-SexyFood ... TOLL FREE

Fax: 1-781-239-8158 (include form)

E-mail: Lorraine@SexyFoodForSingles.com

Cheque ... Money order ... Credit card

Number .... Expiration date ....

@ $12.95 each ..... $_____
Shipping for 1st book $ _3.00_   1st class

For two books $ _3.20_   1st class
Massachusetts residents
please add 5% tax $_____

International $ _7.05_   Air books
For two books $ _11.05_ Air books
                          TOTAL: _____

All prices subject to change.

Name: _____

Address: _____

City: _____ State: _____ Zip: _____

Telephone: _____

Added features:
Autographed by author
For fun: Fortune-telling fish
(while they last)

Want More?

Books ... Books ... Books ...
With Ten (10) New Yorker Cartoons

__Call__: 1-877-SexyFood ... TOLL FREE

__Fax__: 1-781-239-8158 (include form)

__E-mail__: Lorraine@SexyFoodForSingles.com

__Cheque__ ... __Money order__ ... __Credit card__

Number .... Expiration date ....

@ \$12.95 each	\$_____
Shipping for 1st book	\$ _3.00_ 1st class
For two books	\$ _3.20_ 1st class
Massachusetts residents please add 5% tax	\$_____
International	\$ _7.05_ Air books
For two books	\$ _11.05_ Air books
TOTAL: _____	

All prices subject to change.

__Name__: _____

__Address__: _____

__City__: _____ State: _____ Zip: _____

__Telephone__: _____

__Added features__:
Autographed by author
__For fun__: Fortune-telling fish
(while they last)

Want More?

Books ... Books ... Books ...
With Ten (10) New Yorker Cartoons

Call: 1-877-SexyFood ... TOLL FREE

Fax: 1-781-239-8158 (include form)

E-mail: Lorraine@SexyFoodForSingles.com

Cheque ... Money order ... Credit card

Number .... Expiration date ....

@ $12.95 each ..... $_____
Shipping for 1st book $ 3.00   1st class

For two books $ 3.20   1st class
Massachusetts residents
please add 5% tax $_____

International $ 7.05   Air books
For two books $ 11.05   Air books
                    TOTAL: _____

All prices subject to change.

Name: _____

Address: _____

City: _____ State: _____ Zip: _____

Telephone: _____

Added features:
Autographed by author
For fun: Fortune-telling fish
(while they last)

Want More?

Books ... Books ... Books ...
With Ten (10) New Yorker Cartoons

Call: 1-877-SexyFood ... TOLL FREE

Fax: 1-781-239-8158 (include form)

E-mail: Lorraine@SexyFoodForSingles.com

Cheque ... Money order ... Credit card

Number .... Expiration date ....

@ $12.95 each	$_____
Shipping for 1st book	$ _3.00_ 1st class
For two books	$ _3.20_ 1st class
Massachusetts residents please add 5% tax	$_____
International	$ _7.05_ Air books
For two books	$ _11.05_ Air books
	TOTAL: _____

All prices subject to change.

Name: _____

Address: _____

City: _____ State: _____ Zip: _____

Telephone: _____

Added features:
Autographed by author
For fun: Fortune-telling fish
(while they last)

INDEX